I0119414

Habitat

IGNASI RIBÓ

HABITAT

The Ecopolitical Nation

Mycelia Books
London & Barcelona

© 2012 Ignasi Ribó

First Published 2012
by Mycelia Books, London, Great Britain.
All rights reserved.

This book is also published in a variety of electronic formats.
Please visit us at www.myceliabooks.com for more information.

Cover image: Map of Europe and the Mediterranean from a
19th century copy of the *Catalan Atlas*. Drawn in 1375 by
the Majorcan cartographic school and currently held at the
Bibliothèque nationale de France.

British Library Cataloguing in Publication Data
Ribo, Ignasi, 1971-
  Habitat : the ecopolitical nation.
  1. State, The. 2. Liberalism.
  I. Title
  320.1'01-dc23

ISBN: 978-0-9574191-0-0 (paperback)
ISBN: 978-0-9574191-1-7 (ebook)

For Kaew

Contents

About this Book

This book has grown out of a previous one, written in Catalan, *De la indignació a la nació* ("From indignation to nation"), which was published on September 11th 2012, the same day that hundreds of thousands of Catalans took to the streets of Barcelona to demand their freedom and a state of their own.

It was in that book that I first developed the ecopolitical theory and the notion of the habitat-nation that I am exposing here to English readers. The original aim of my reflections was to displace the old ideology of the nation-state, which is still very much divisive in Catalonia, and to ground the nation on a new, more inclusive theoretical framework in which all individuals, regardless of their culture, their origin or their condition, even their species, could find their place in the political community and contribute to the sustainability of common habitation.

By its own nature, the ecopolitical project is not restricted to the transformation of a particular social community such as Catalonia, but aspires to become a model of universal appeal, albeit always within the limits and the possibilities of each specific community. My theory, therefore, rather than offering ready-made institutional solutions that could be indiscriminately applied to all social communities, attempts to set up the foundations that would allow these communities, if they so wish, to constitute themselves as habitat-nations and to develop their own ecopolitical institutions according to their habits and forms of habitation. For the same reason, the theory of the habitat-nation avoids any ideological or partisan ascription, focusing instead on the elaboration of a constitutional framework that could be accepted and assumed by all inhabitants regardless of their inclinations, values or political preferences.

In my previous book, I delved in much more detail into the practical implications of the theory presented here, putting forward specific mechanisms and institutions that could serve to implement the ecopolitical notions in the future state of Catalonia. While many of these reflections and proposals, which touched on political, economic and social issues in considerable depth, might be of some interest to non-Catalan readers, I have decided to exclude them from this book in order to concentrate on the more general proposals of the ecopolitical theory. As a consequence, the reader might feel that my ideas are not sufficiently fleshed out, but tend to linger for too long on the high spheres of theory. I have nothing to say against this criticism, except to invite the critics to undertake the work of elaborating those specific proposals, adapting and developing the concepts discussed in this book to meet the needs and the possibilities of their own habitat-nations. After all, a book should strive to create a sense of wonder and inspire readers to seek their own solutions to the problems, rather than giving them a creed to follow.

Whatever the actual institutions that may eventually stem from it, an unavoidable conclusion from my theory is the urgent need to redefine the geopolitical units that make up the current world, abandoning once and for all the model of the nation-state and advancing towards more ecologically and socially sustainable political communities. This book attempts to justify, both theoretically and practically, why this process is so necessary and how it could be accomplished in the present political context. But surely, as always, the world is already running ahead of our theories. The rusted structures of the nation-states, particularly the largest ones, are already showing evident signs of decay and instability. New habitat-nations may be about to achieve statehood, both in Europe and in America. A new world seems to be forging its way ahead. Let us hope that it will be so organised that we shall not regret calling it our home.

October 2012

1 The Bear and the Stork: a Fable

W e the living are very often trapped, by the same nature of our consciousness, in the illusion of a present that seems immutable. The political structures that surround us, and to a large extent rule our lives, acquire then the consistency of natural phenomena. Nothing that we might do or refrain from doing would seem capable of transforming, much less overturning, institutions so seemingly solid that many would take them as eternal. And yet, change is inherent in all human institutions, even in those that attempt to clench more firmly to their own persistence. When we take a look at the large states that still dominate international politics and we ponder whether it will be really possible for a new, better world to emerge from our present situation, we would do well to remember the fable of the bear and the stork.

For more than forty years, the entire world lived under the impression that the Cold War, the territorial confrontation between the capitalist and the communist blocks, was a permanent fact of life, not much more alterable than the rain or the cyclones. The Union of Soviet Socialist Republics in particular seemed to be an entity destined to outlast many human generations, even the end of history according to some. In just a few months, however, this immense military and territorial unit made up of twenty or so republics and satellite states crumbled like a sandcastle leaving almost no trace of its previous existence. Many reasons have been advanced to explain the sudden collapse of the Soviet block, a revolution that no one expected and which has profoundly transformed the geopolitical structure of the whole of Europe, and indeed the world. It is often assumed that the great victor of the Cold War, and ultimately the cause of the Soviet Union's disintegration, was the capitalist system. There is no doubt that the liberal democracies of the West and their economic model, as well as the internal transformations encouraged by Soviet leaders, were key factors in the events that led to the fall of the Berlin Wall and to the breakup of the Warsaw Pact. It is often forgotten, however, that the main force that caused such a rapid decomposition was not Western pressure, but the struggle for independence of some small nations, particularly Lithuania and the other Baltic states, which frustrated the hopes of a partial reform of the communist system. These revolts, like the ones in the Czech Republic, Slovakia, Hungary, Poland and elsewhere, were marked not so much by the demand of economic prosperity or a Western system of government, but by the aspiration of each one of these nations to organise by themselves their political community, free from the interference of any foreign power. In many places, such as in Estonia and Latvia, the resistance of these small nations was grounded from the beginning on the defence of the nation's ecosystems, the air and the water, the animals and the plants, which the large state had been mishandling for years by indiscriminately exploiting natural resources, setting up huge power plants or filling the rivers with its endless waste. The Lithuanians forming a human chain to stop Soviet tanks is therefore an example, not of the struggle for a capitalistic world, but of the struggle for a world of habitat-nations. The inhabitants of the small nations of eastern Europe stood up to the large Russian bear, risking their own lives and the lives of their loved ones, not because they wanted better appliances, but because they aspired to live in a community of free inhabitants, founded on the sustainability of cohabitation and on the principles of justice. These revolutions, like Lithuania's storks, carry perhaps in their beak the habitat-nations that are yet to be born.

2

What is a Habitat-nation?

A nation, like nature, is only meaningful in so far as it allows the regeneration of the conditions of life from life itself. All human inhabitants are born into a biological and a social community, and we cannot isolate ourselves from these communities except by the conceptual violence of our abstractions. We all have a home, and this home is not just the natural habitat where we find our subsistence, but also the community that we constitute with the other inhabitants, with whom we share habits and forms of habitation. Inhabitants, by definition, cohabit and sustain each other in order to preserve and regenerate the natural conditions of this cohabitation. Nature, as the complex articulation of the biological community, does not require any human intervention to sustain itself, to be constantly born and reborn according to its own capacities. But the nation, as the articulation of the social community, can only be regenerated if humans are able to sustain the institutions, the practices and the principles that allow them to live together. Without the social habits of human beings such as autonomy, reciprocity and friendship, it would not be possible, at least in principle, to develop any form of political community in our planet. These habits, however, do not ensure that these meaningful political communities, the nations, will have sufficient ecological and social coherence to sustain a society organised according to the principles of justice. The habitat-nation, founded on the common good of the sustainability of cohabitation, is a model of articulation of the political community that effectively extends the rights and duties of liberty, fairness and care to all inhabitants regardless of gender, age, culture, origin or species. Only inhabitants, in so far as they deliberately choose to live together, are legitimised to organise themselves politically and to develop the political, economic and social institutions of the habitat-nation.

The habitat-nation, as defined in this book, is thus the community of individuals (inhabitants) who share a way of being, due to the confluence of genetically and socially acquired dispositions (habits), as well as the set of strategies, practices and institutions (forms of habitation) that allow them to adapt to (inhabit) a given natural environment (habitat) in a sustainable manner, thanks to the bonds of autonomy, reciprocity and friendship.

What is a Habitat-nation?

The following pages attempt to give an adequate justification to this definition, as well as exposing its relevance for the articulation of the political community in today's world. Once these questions have been answered, however, our task will have only begun. Regardless of its theoretical justification, the habitat-nation will be no more than an empty shell if we, the inhabitants, do not adopt it as a project worth pursuing in our own social and biological communities. It is by undertaking the task of building effective communities of free inhabitants that each one of us will be able to answer the truly significant question: how do I want *my own* habitat-nation to be?

3

Habit or the Animal

We are animals. However simple, this fact is often overlooked by political theories. *Homo sapiens* is thus presented as a strange kind of creature, an exception in the animal kingdom, a species conditioned only by its free will and by the workings of its unique capacity for culture. Any suggestion that instincts or genetics might also have some influence on its behaviour is often met with an almost fanatical contempt. Human beings, it is claimed, are "socially constructed" and they are not subject to hereditary factors, not enough at least to condition in any meaningful way their behaviour. If this denial of human nature is so common in today's world, against all scientific and common sense evidence, it is because many people need to believe that those human behaviours that are morally offensive, such as murder or rape, can be eradicated once and for all, either by an effort of the will or through a general transformation of society's cultural make-up. Nothing could be further from the truth.

What we can gather from the ethnological understanding of human beings, as well as from the ethological understanding of animals in general, is that culture is not opposed in any way to nature, but rather they are both part of the same continuum. The wonderful plasticity and adaptability of human culture is not the proof that *homo sapiens* has somehow crossed an invisible boundary between nature and society, leaving behind a humiliating dependence on the mechanics of instincts to embrace the life of the soul. What it shows, rather, is that natural selection has pushed it to develop an extraordinarily effective instrument to deal with the challenges of its environment and thrive as a species. Socialisation, learning and all the other mechanisms that sociologists tend to magnify do not act upon an amorphous and blank matter, but upon innate dispositions, physical and mental structures that have evolved together with culture and cannot be understood without it. Nature and culture can only be separated in our concepts. Even then it is hardly possible to establish with any certainty where one begins and the other one ends. A human being without culture is nothing; and culture without human nature is no more than an abstraction of philosophers.

In spite of its limited explanatory value, social constructivism remains the dominant paradigm in today's humanities and social sciences. Granted that many human realities are, at least in part, socially constructed, this pre-eminence may be to a certain extent justified. Too often, however, the hypothesis that some human realities are socially constructed gives way to the dogma that all human reality is socially constructed. It is in this ideological context that any insinuation that may limit in some way human freedom, whether at the individual or the collective level, finds a stiff resistance from intellectuals and activists. Inflamed by a crusader's zeal, the defenders of the social malleability of human beings often react against heretics with the fury of organised religions. What these progressive militants fear is that accepting the notion that human nature is conditioned by the evolutionary process may end up undermining the notions of individual and collective responsibility that seem to sustain human progress and the whole edifice of morals. The democratic value of equality, for instance, would seem to be threatened if we were to accept that there are innate differences amongst people. Some fear that Social Darwinism or even racism may become once again generally accepted doctrines. But the notion of equality and the politics that are derived from it have never been based on an identity between individuals or human groups. Rather, they are based on the recognition of an equal dignity for all, regardless of gender, skin colour, IQ or any other personal trait. Denying those differences does not contribute in any way to the politics of integration and equality, just as denying the innate tendency of males to exert sexual violence does not contribute to effectively protect the females of the species. The problem is the confusion between facts and values, as well as a collective inability to develop the latter from the former, instead of bending the former to make them fit the latter. The outcome of this Procrustean practice is a political culture founded on narratives that may be encouraging and gratifying, but are no more realistic than fairy tales.

There is no denying that social conditions and a certain amount of individual freedom affect the way human beings behave. Many opportunities for social reform and human advancement are thus open. But neither the autonomy of the individual nor the autonomy of culture should be overstretched in order to deny the inherited dispositions of human nature, much less to promote projects of social engineering. Like all other animal species, *homo sapiens* is conditioned to a large extent by its biological make-up, by its innate mental structures and by its genes, which are the outcome of a protracted evolutionary process. The degree in which innate, social and subjective motivations interact to form human behaviour is of course an active field of research. What we cannot continue to accept are the self-satisfying fictions that defend an irreducible autonomy of the subject or promote some form of social determinism based on the dogmatic denial of human nature. Even when inspired by the best of intentions this kind of fiction, like the ones that sustained in the past geocentricism or the great chain of being, can only beget monsters. As a French proverb says, "chase nature out of the door, she will rush back in through the window".

Like all species that inhabit the planet, from the smallest to the largest, the human animal is the product of a complex evolutionary process that has multiplied and diversified the genetic configurations of individuals and populations under the pressure of environmental conditions. In all organisms the basic mechanism of adaptation is the natural selection of the genomic variants of the fittest individuals, in so far as they are able to increase their ability to produce more offspring. These mechanisms of Darwinian evolution, at least in their general terms, have now been substantiated with a considerable amount of evidence. There are, however, certain organisms, like some birds and some social mammals, particularly the great apes, which have evolved forms of interaction with the environment and between themselves that seem to escape the purely biological mechanisms. Whether these forms of interaction correspond to the concept of culture or whether culture is an exclusive trait of humans is still a bitter subject of debate amongst scientists and philosophers. Leaving aside these debates, marked too often by the anthropocentric prejudice, it seems quite obvious that at least one of these great apes, *homo sapiens*, has developed during its evolutionary process the capacity to manipulate, store and distribute information through mechanisms of social interaction. Indeed, humans are cultural animals.

But perhaps we should not be overly proud of it. After all, culture is no more than a biological adaptation of humans, just as echolocation is a biological adaptation of bats. Unlike other adaptations, however, culture has unintended consequences for the evolutionary process, to the extent that it interacts continuously and effectively with the natural selection of genetic variants. Humans learn from each other, innovate from what they have learned and convey these innovations to their offspring. This process of cultural accumulation allows the species to adapt rapidly to all kinds of environments, even to alter them substantially to meet its own needs. *Homo sapiens* has thus been able to spread across the planet and has developed forms of habitation that are extraordinarily complex, even if not always fully adaptive. Later I will discuss in more detail these dynamics of habitation; here I only want to stress the fact that human behaviour stems from two interlaced processes: genetic evolution and cultural evolution.

The best way to understand this confluence of nature (genetic transmission of information) and culture (social transmission of information) is through the concept of "habit". We all have habits. These are not just behaviours, but certain patterns of behaviour that tend to recur and which we cannot fully control. Indeed, most often we are not even aware of our own habits. Where do these habits come from? And how do they define our way of being? It is clear that habits are not just physical or mental, but they are not purely cultural either. We walk in a certain way, we talk in a certain way, and we eat in a certain way. We haven't just learned all these patterns of behaviour, although the culture that surrounds us, our social environment, has definitely conditioned them. We haven't just inherited them either, although our genetic make-up, the biological structures of our body and our mind, have definitely conditioned them. As the underlying patterns of our behaviour, habits precede all representations, values and ideas that constitute the visible aspect of culture. But they are not just instructions coded on our DNA, like scripts to be parsed and executed by our central processing unit. In our habits, nature and culture, innate information and social information are bundled together in a seamless pattern. It is not just our behaviour, but our way of being in the world that is defined by these patterns of genetically and socially acquired information. Individuals, and indeed whole groups, act in response to a particular environment, but their behaviour, far from being totally contingent, stems from dispositions that have become permanently embedded in their being as habits. We can thus define a habit as an individual's or a group's way of being, due to the confluence of genetically and socially acquired dispositions. We should probably aim for a more precise definition, but this one provides us for the moment with an intuitively sound concept that reflects the existence of certain deep and permanent dispositions, which are not exactly behaviours, but bring about behaviours when individuals and groups, both human and non-human, interact with their natural or social environment. There is no need, therefore, for any metaphysical notion of character, essence, spirit or soul. Habits are not entities, but patterns formed through multiple and complex interactions between individuals and social groups.

Now that we have defined the concept, we need to better understand its variability. It is quite obvious that different human groups have different habits. Moreover, within a particular human group there are habits shared by all individuals and habits that are peculiar to some individuals or subgroups. Social scientists have been struggling for a long time to determine the relative importance of cultural, genetic and environmental factors in the formation of human behaviour. In the face of the obvious diversity of human societies, many anthropologists tend to explain behaviour as a product of culture (social constructivism is an extreme example of this tendency). Psychologists and biologists, on the other hand, working more often than not with transcultural samples of populations and large statistical models, tend to give much more importance to genes or other innate factors (some may even deny that culture has any kind of influence on behaviour at all). Finally, sociologists and geographers, who are usually interested in the local processes of adaptation, tend to stress environmental factors as the key component of behaviour As in the old Indian story of the three blind men and the elephant, every specialist describes a different animal, when in fact they are all feeling it from their own particular perspective. But if we want to reconstruct the whole animal, we need to do more than just combine these partial descriptions. We need to understand more precisely where the differences and the similarities that constitute it originate from.

What we would need to find out is whether people's habits vary because they have inherited different genes, because they have acquired different knowledge, values and attitudes, or because they have lived in different environments. I will deal with this last factor later on, as it doesn't usually have a direct effect on behaviour, but tends to influence it through processes of biological or cultural adaptation. If we concentrate strictly on habits, we have to recognise that they are conditioned both by nature and by culture. But how do we explain the fact that there are so many differences in habits between groups and within groups?

What many studies have shown in recent years is that genetic factors are largely irrelevant when attempting to explain the differences in habits amongst human groups. Differences between individuals of the same group, on the other hand, seem to respond equally to genetic factors and non-shared cultural or environmental factors. This is easy to understand if we bear in mind that the genetic variance on a sample of human individuals representative of different cultures is very small, even if some superficial aspects of their phenotype (skin tone, eye colour, hair texture) may lead us to think otherwise. If we take a sample of individuals from the same cultural group, however, all systematic cultural factors are no longer relevant since all the individuals share them, and therefore genetic factors become quite significant (50%). Another important point is that, against all common sense, the non-shared cultural factors that explain the remaining 50% of variability between individuals of the same group are not transmitted within the family, but rather through learning and imitation of role models in the context of larger social environments such as the school, networks of friends or the media. In order to avoid misunderstandings, it is important to stress that we are referring here to factors that explain the differences between individuals, not to the absolute influences on individual traits. From an statistical point of view, family upbringing has little or no effect on the differences in habits amongst individuals of the same social group.

Both sets of factors, genetic and cultural, make up an individual's habits; but the differences in habit between individuals are basically cultural, derived from the general culture of the group or the specific subcultures to which they have been exposed. Genetic variability between human groups is thus negligible.

This is hardly surprising taking into account that humans have adapted to their different habitats through mechanisms of cultural evolution. Without its extraordinary capacity for cultural accumulation and diversification, it is quite likely that *homo sapiens*, confronted with so many different environments, would have split into several biological species a long time ago. Of course, without culture it would not have been able to spread so successfully in the first place. In summary, differences between human populations are basically cultural, while similarities are mostly genetic. The great variety of human cultures studied by anthropologists is certainly real, but no less than the universal traits that all these groups share thanks to their common genetic inheritance. Unity and diversity are just two sides of the same elephant.

Some universal traits of humans, such as their aggressiveness, competitiveness or individualism, are well known and widely documented. These traits are not, however, exclusively human but are shared in one way or another by almost all species of social animals. Therefore, they must have some adaptive function that has allowed them to evolve under the pressure of natural selection. It is not hard to see that all these behaviours help individuals to get ahead in the struggle for survival and reproduction, particularly in social contexts where scarce resources such as territory, prey, status or mates are intensely disputed by the different members of the group and by other groups of the same species. Individuals who are able to gain an advantage in this competition will tend to have more offspring, and those genes that condition "egoistic" habits will tend to spread at the expense of the more "altruistic" ones. There is no need for genetics, however, to recognise here the old picture of human beings engaged in a war of all against all, which has often been used to justify the need for a strong central authority that would protect them against their neighbours. These same traits have also underpinned the theory of capitalism, which trusts the common well-being on the automatic adjustment of the selfish interests of individuals through the invisible hand of the market. It is quite evident, nonetheless, that this description of humans as optimisers of individual performance, still prevalent in many contemporary economic and political models, is far from being an accurate picture of the species. There are other crucial traits of humans, such as their moral sentiments, their tendency to cooperate in order to achieve common ends and their capacity to sacrifice themselves for the good of others, that are generally ignored by the "selfish animal" storyline. These cooperative habits are also part of the genetic make-up of many social animals and must therefore have an adaptive value just as relevant as the more individualistic habits. But altruistic and cooperative behaviours, which are especially significant in the case of humans, cannot be easily explained in strictly Darwinian terms. This difficulty has inspired an intense and often controversial research effort on the part of ethologists, psychologists and economists who have undertaken the task of unravelling the evolutionary origins of human altruism. Not until recently, however, has the picture of humans as a fundamentally cooperative species begun to displace the still dominant theories of the *homo economicus.*

Besides ethnographic and common sense observations, the most interesting empirical evidence on the prosocial habits of humans comes from several experiments conducted by economists in the past few years. The subjects of these experiments interact anonymously in different kinds of games that confront them with the so-called problems of collective action such as the prisoner's dilemma, the sharing of public goods or the exchange of gifts. Far from showing an overwhelmingly selfish human being, these experiments tend to demonstrate that people have social dispositions that cannot be explained in strictly individualistic terms. I cannot discuss here these results in any depth, but I will try to summarise very briefly the most relevant conclusions:

(1) individuals seem to have a general inclination to reciprocate or cooperate with others beyond their own interest;

(2) this reciprocity is never absolute, but is always mixed with some degree of selfishness;

(3) individuals are more or less inclined to cooperate depending on psychological and cultural factors that are hard to determine with precision;

(4) the degree and the mechanism of this reciprocity depends strongly on the cultural and institutional context where the experiment is conducted;

(5) reciprocity is significantly higher when individuals have a sense of belonging to the same group (even if the group is artificially marked);

(6) individuals adjust their level of reciprocity according to the attitude of the other participants and tend to punish non-cooperative behaviours (free-riders);

(7) reciprocity increases substantially when participants have been able to agree beforehand on the rules and the punishments that will regulate the group's interaction (a social contract of sorts).

In order to place these results within their theoretical context, we should distinguish two forms of cooperative behaviour: mutualism and altruism. In both instances, individuals who cooperate in some activity have common benefits and individual costs derived from this cooperation. In mutualism, as in trade or other commercial relationships, the net result for all individual participants is potentially positive and the behaviour can be easily explained as an enlarged form of egoism. There are many situations, however, where cooperation is likely to impose net costs on some individuals in the form of direct costs or a decrease in life chances; and yet many individuals still choose to cooperate. Just think of the classic example of the man who jumps into the sea to save a drowning stranger; altruism refers to this form of apparently unselfish cooperation between individuals. The question that intrigues biologists and has been the object of passionate debates in recent years is whether this altruistic inclination of humans has actually been able to evolve under the pressure of natural selection. In a specific social context, it would seem that selfish behaviours (free-riders) have an evolutionary advantage, as they are able to profit from cooperation without paying the costs. In the long term, the "asocial" genes should thus spread through the population, until they have effectively wiped out their "prosocial" competitors. But this is not what we observe. In actual populations there is a variable combination of egoistic and altruistic behaviours - how should we explain it?

Altruism between members of the same family, so-called nepotistic altruism, can be readily explained in evolutionary terms if we take into account that close relatives share to some extent the same genes. Individual who sacrifice themselves for the sake of their relatives could be enhancing their own fitness, or rather the fitness of the genes that they have in common with their relatives. Of course, we are speaking here of the ultimate causes of individual behaviour, not of their proximate or psychological motivations. An extreme case of this type of cooperation is found in social insects, like ants, bees or termites, whose colonies are in effect large families with very close genetic ties. Without reaching this same degree of integration, there is no doubt that the intensity of family ties in humans and other mammals, as well as the feelings associated with them, have been able to evolve to some degree because the genes that motivate them benefit from family cooperation and tend therefore to spread through populations.

Another type of altruism that may be explained in egoistic terms is reciprocal altruism or weak reciprocity, which is in fact a complex and deferred form of mutualism. In the context of small social groups with recurrent interactions, even if there was no genetic relationship between individuals, altruism could still have evolved through the exchange of favours. As long as groups are small and members are able to recognise each other, individuals who sacrifice themselves for fellow members can expect them to reciprocate and sacrifice themselves in return sometime in the future. Certain theoretical models explain the evolution of all altruistic inclinations in humans as a result of this kind of weak reciprocity, which would have allowed the development and spread of cooperation beyond family groups in the early populations of hominids.

By itself, however, reciprocal altruism does not give a satisfactory explanation of the fact that cooperation in humans is so widespread, embracing very large groups where personal interactions are limited and the hope of future reciprocation of favours is extraordinarily uncertain. As many experiments and field observations have shown, humans display prosocial behaviours even when they have no motive whatsoever to expect a future benefit, sometimes even when they know for certain that cooperation will impose on them a direct cost. It is this social disposition of individuals, their social habits, that sustains the collective norms on which the large cooperative projects that characterise human sociability are built. It is not yet clear whether these dispositions, as well as the "moral sentiments" that are usually attached to them, derive in some way from nepotistic and reciprocal altruism, or whether they stem directly from a process of cultural and genetic coevolution which may have furthered strong reciprocity amongst the foraging bands of early humans. This is no doubt an important question which will probably continue to spark lively debates in the near future. For our purposes, however, it is enough to acknowledge that human cooperative habits are not irrational tendencies, but have a definite adaptive value, in so far as they enhance the fitness of individuals that are part of groups where these habits are more prevalent. Throughout evolution human groups have naturally tended to promote and consolidate these cooperative habits by implementing norms and institutions that punish asocial behaviours, encourage a fair distribution of the benefits of social cooperation and strengthen the group's internal cohesion against other groups that compete for the same resources. This is one of the reasons why humans have evolved such a strong group mentality, with a marked tendency to cooperate within their own group and to compete or fight against other groups, often through very violent means.

The interest of individuals and the interest of the group appear thus to be interlaced in a complex social system that has evolved genetically and culturally through hundreds of thousands of years and has never been without conflicts and tensions. Human sociability is the result of this confluence of habits, egoistic and altruistic, exploitative and cooperative; and we will not be able to get rid of one or the other. The liberal, or rather libertarian, vision of a *homo economicus* freed from the ties of reciprocity is so unreal as the utopian attempts to extirpate or suppress selfishness from individuals in order to achieve social harmony. Informed of the nature of human habits, we should recognise that a well-ordered society is founded at the same time on the respect of individual freedoms and on the strengthening of the ties of reciprocity.

4 Habitation or Dwelling

Around fifty thousand years ago, a small group of modern humans emigrated from the African savannah and began to colonise distant lands. Since then, we have evolved genetically and culturally in order to adapt to the requirements of such diverse environments as Australian deserts, Polynesian archipelagos, European valleys, American prairies or Siberian taigas, amongst many others. No other species, except perhaps for rats and some microbes, has been able to establish itself permanently in such a wide range of habitats and in such a short span of time. The ability to accumulate cultural innovations has been the key factor that has allowed humans to spread so rapidly across the world. With a population of more than 7 billion and an extraordinarily powerful technology, *homo sapiens* has now become the driving force behind the climatic and ecological changes that affect the planet. Some scientists have already described our time as the Anthropocene, a new geological era dominated by human intervention on every ecosystem and on the whole of the biosphere. Many are wondering, however, if humans are really capable of exercising this dominance responsibly. Perhaps we are nothing more than a bunch of apes who have stolen the keys to the lab and will not stop until it blows up in our faces.

In order to judge our present situation and the possible consequences for the future, it is essential that we grasp the process through which *homo sapiens* has been able to occupy all the inhabitable areas of the planet and to economically exploit almost all the rest. We can begin by defining "habitation" as the set of strategies, practices and institutions that allow the adaptation of a group to a given natural environment (habitat). According to evolutionary theory, an adaptation is no more than the ability of an organism to adjust to the changes in its environment in order to increase its fitness. In the specific case of *homo sapiens*, its adaptive strategies are particularly complex, flexible and effective. Not only do they include variations in behaviour (short term adaptation) and genetic variations (long term adaptation), but also all those cultural variations that are accumulated in the social group (medium term adaptation). Humans adjust their behaviour to their environment, but they are also capable of adjusting their environment to their behaviour. All other animals, of course, modify the environment with their actions, but none of them is able to transform it so thoroughly and permanently as humans. The difference, once again, is the exceptional ability of our species to manipulate, accumulate and distribute information through the mechanisms of social interaction. The global expansion of *homo sapiens* cannot be understood without taking into account this capacity for cultural accumulation, which in turn has restrained, without eliminating it altogether, the effect of natural selection on its genetic variability. But how, under which conditions and through which specific methods, has this process of human habitation of the different ecosystems of the earth actually taken place?

Traditionally, the study of human habitation has been split between two conflicting hypotheses: environmental determinism and possibilism. Human ecologists have often defended the idea that the natural conditions of the environment (climate, soil, landscape, geology, vegetation, etc.) are determinant factors in the evolution of the different strategies, practices and institutions that characterise the forms of human habitation. Cultural anthropologists, on the other hand, tend to defend the idea that nature is just a general backstage where the different human possibilities are unwrapped following the traditions, value systems and other historical peculiarities of each culture. An example might help to illustrate this all-too-academic debate. If a group of Polynesians were to arrive at an inhabited coast of Greenland and had to settle there, which forms of habitation would they end up developing, similar to their Inuit neighbours or closer to their Polynesian ancestors? The answer, as usual, is somewhere between these two extremes. It is quite likely that this hypothetical society of Arctic Polynesians would have to develop strategies of subsistence adapted to their new environment and thus very different from the strategies of their ancestors. At the same time, the social institutions and cultural practices that would allow them to organise the new habitation are likely to be conditioned by their own traditions and thus differ significantly from the institutions and practices of their neighbours. Needless to say, cases like this one, albeit perhaps not so extreme, have been quite common throughout history as populations have often emigrated or colonised distant territories. Wherever humans have had to adapt to new environments, the group's cultural traditions have clearly shaped the particular forms of habitation. This is hardly surprising if we consider that human groups, far from building their dwellings as a rational response to the conditions of the environment, commonly exploit their accumulated traditions as a heuristic guide that allows them to meet the challenges of environmental change. This cultural inertia is often a good adaptive strategy, especially where the new environment is not so different from the previous one and the group has the ability to modify it to a certain extent. Thus, the Greek colonists who founded new cities throughout the

Mediterranean tended to bring with them many of their traditional forms of habitation and their cultural practices, even if they had to adjust their modes of production somewhat in order to thrive in the new natural environments where they settled. The fact that many of these Greek contributions such as the cultivation of vine and olive trees have outlasted their carriers is lively proof of the relevance of cultural inertia in the processes of human habitation. In general, human groups are quite capable of adapting their forms of dwelling to their particular environment, while preserving at the same time their own habits and accumulated cultural traditions. This tendency to rely both on the environment and on history does not always have adaptive results, but in most cases, if we have to judge by the success of the species, it turns out well enough. In simple terms, we could say that the natural habitat sets the limits and the strategic possibilities, while history defines the actual practices and institutions. Both of these conditions, in any case, give rise to the specific habits and forms of habitation that allow human groups to adapt to their environments through biological as well as social adjustments.

These forms of social organisation can be explained by the fact that any population, in order to survive and thrive in the long term, needs to manage the material and energetic resources available in its habitat in the most efficient way. The modes of acquisition and production of food in particular are very much dependent on the possibilities and conditions of the natural environment, at least in those contexts where few external factors alter this dependency. Ecological anthropologists often classify the modes of subsistence according to the specific strategies followed by the different human groups in order to satisfy their food requirements. These basic modes of production are hunting and gathering, horticulture, agriculture, and pastoralism. Without the need to postulate any kind of determinism, it is obvious that the forms of habitation are strongly conditioned by these subsistence strategies. Hunters and gatherers tend to develop nomadic forms of habitation, linked to the seasonal availability of resources and to the natural regeneration of their habitat. Horticulturalists, on the other hand, dwell longer on their habitat, although not always permanently, since they need to invest time and resources on the active production of food through slash-and-burn agriculture or some other form of extensive cultivation. Personal and collective investment in the land becomes much more substantial in agricultural societies, which tend to establish themselves permanently and develop stable forms of habitation with significant increases in population and a constant intervention on the ecological structure of their habitat. Finally, pastoralists must also manage intensively their natural resources, but they tend towards nomadic forms of habitation, dependent on the displacement of domesticated livestock through arid or semi-arid environments where the access to water or pasture is often unstable. In reality, of course, these modes of production, in so far as they constitute ideal types, are almost never found in a pure form. Every human group develops its own particular strategies of subsistence and modes of habitation adapted to the specific conditions of its environment. These strategies are always embedded in forms of social organisation and cultural practices which aim not only to obtain the maximum energetic yield from the habitat, but also to foster other human needs (affective, moral, aesthetic) and to improve the resilience of the group in front of unexpected environmental changes.

If the processes of habitation responded only to the natural characteristics of the habitat, it would be difficult to explain why human populations have adapted in so many different ways to the same kinds of habitat and in similar ways to different kinds of habitat. It is quite obvious that all these adaptations have been also conditioned by factors that could be defined as historical, such as technological and cultural innovation, social change, epidemics, displacement of populations, new forms of energy or trading routes. While many of these factors are at least in part determined by the environment, their effect on human habitation is often contingent and cannot be reduced to the simple logic of functionalism. These effects have been, in any case, quite significant throughout history. From the diffusion of agriculture during the Neolithic to the current process of globalisation, widespread historical events and processes have frequently unsettled the modes of subsistence, cultural practices and social institutions of the different human groups. The patterns and routes of trade, for instance, have had a deep influence on the forms of habitation of those groups that have been able to profit from them in order to develop far beyond what they could have hoped to achieve with their own resources. The dispersion of technological innovations through these routes, often constrained by geographical accidents or bioclimatic boundaries, has driven the processes of expansion, conquest and colonisation that fill up the pages of history. The industrial revolution that has transformed the productive capacity of humans in the last three centuries cannot be understood without taking into account these dynamics of technological diffusion, but also the fortuitous discovery of vast, albeit finite, deposits of fossil fuels. At the same time, this expansion of industrial output and international trade, usually summed up under the concept of globalisation, has deeply unsettled the forms of habitation of almost every population on the planet, leaving aside a few and ever decreasing groups of isolated aborigines. In the wake of contacts with international economic agents, many traditional societies have had to modify, often against their will, their systems of subsistence in order to adapt to the expansion of trade relationships, the sudden intensification of agricultural production, the introduction of paid work, the loss of natural resources or the penetration of new cultivars, amongst other external factors. It is quite obvious, therefore, that history has conditioned the different forms of human habitation at least as much as the natural environment, although it has not always done so in an adaptive sense. Unlike the strict ecological limits imposed by the environment, even as humans actively intervene to modify it, historical factors have tended to promote forms of habitation, like urbanism or industrial consumerism, that undermine the human habitat and the ecosystem as a whole.

In ecological terms, an ecosystem is simply a biological community (animals, plants, fungi and microorganisms) together with all the abiotic elements (air, energy, chemicals, geological structures, man-made structures) that surround them. Ecosystems function as an integrated whole in space and time, woven by the cycles of energy, materials and information that interconnect the different elements of the system. The biological community, in particular, is fundamentally linked by the food web, which is characterised by the fact that some organisms acquire energy from the abiotic environment (autotrophs), while some acquire it by eating or decomposing other organisms (heterotrophs). Ecosystems are usually formed through a process known as community assembly, whereby the different organisms successively join the biological community, in so far as the physical conditions of the environment and the chances of survival and reproduction allow them to effectively cohabit with the rest of organisms. Each species adopts a certain function within the ecosystem, occupying a particular ecological niche and interacting with the other species through complex strategies of predation, competition and symbiosis. These interrelations, far from being fixed, are subject to processes of coadaptation and coevolution, through which the different organisms of the biological community tend to accommodate each other, both in the short and the long term. Predators and prey, for instance, are constantly rebalancing each other through the dynamics of predation and competitive evolution. Hence, their populations tend to stay within the limits of the carrying capacity of their habitat. It is precisely this sort of interaction between organisms that gives the system its capacity to self-regulate (or self-organise) through positive and negative feedback loops. This capacity, more than just summing up the individual elements and events, constitutes an emerging property of the ecosystem. Not unlike the homoeostatic regulation of an organisms' physiology, natural ecosystems tend towards equilibrium by themselves. It is nonetheless a dynamic equilibrium, a fragile balance that is always vulnerable to the processes of ecological succession, which may arise from internal changes in the system but also from external shocks. In general, a mature ecosystem is able to remain in this steady state for centuries, until a sufficiently large disruption such as a fire or a hurricane sets it once again out of balance.

How does human habitation fit into these natural (self-regulated) ecosystems? And what kinds of man-made ecosystems (partially or totally regulated by humans) are produced in the course of this habitation? To a certain extent, human populations interact with their ecosystems in a very similar manner to other animal species. Humans occupy a particular ecological niche, typically at the top of the food chain. The human social system (culture, technology, social organisation) is thus integrated in the ecosystem through constant flows of materials, energy and information that circulate in both directions. Not unlike the rest of species, the human social system evolves and adapts to the other elements of the ecosystem, in the same way that these elements evolve and adapt to the human social system. The different forms of human habitation, particularly in pre-industrial cultures, are clearly marked by this process of coevolution and coadaptation, in so far as they grow out of many generations of human cohabitation with a particular biological community. At the same time, humans are always dependent on their ecosystem for food and other basic resources such as air, water, minerals or shelter. These ecosystem services are often renewable, as human waste returns to the system and is recycled by the different elements of the biological community thanks to the bountiful supply of solar energy. Human habitation is so closely linked with the cycles of materials and energy which regulate the natural ecosystem that a serious disruption of these cycles can render any human habitat inhabitable. Unlike other animals, though, humans have been able to alter their habitat very substantially and have even created new ecosystems, whose regulation depends to a large extent on their own activities. The agricultural ecosystems, designed and managed by the human populations that inhabit them, can only be sustained by a constant and active intervention of humans over the autonomous processes of nature. In order to sustain these ecosystems, a considerable amount of additional resources, whether in the form of work, materials or energy, needs to be deployed. Before the development of industrial agriculture, the limited availability of resources and the different forms of polyculture ensured that many of these ecosystems were managed in a fairly sustainable manner, even if the cases of mismanagement and over-exploitation of resources have never been lacking. In the case of urban ecosystems, environmental imbalances tend to be even greater, given that cities are inhabited almost exclusively by humans who need therefore to pull in great quantities of external resources and to throw out similar quantities of waste which cannot be recycled internally. It is quite evident that no human habitation could ever last if it had to rely exclusively on artificial ecosystems, whether agricultural or urban.

These forms of habitation have only been able to develop in the context of larger natural ecosystems which have generally served as a source of materials and energy, as well as a sink for waste products. The active management of these mixed environments, also called mosaic landscapes, has allowed human populations, both ancient and modern, to build up complex social systems characterised quite often, but not always, by sustainable environmental practices.

It is a common mistake to think that human habitation has only turned maladaptive with the expansion of industrial civilisation. Certainly in the past three hundred years or so, technological innovation, urban sprawl and fossil fuel consumption have significantly worsened the magnitude and scale of the ecological problems. And there is no doubt that the uncontrolled growth of the human population is driving many species to extinction and producing alterations in the ecosystems, such as climate change, which may be irreversible. A brief glance at human history, however, shows that there have been many instances in the past where populations have not been able, or have not been willing, to respect the ecological constraints of their own habitats. In some of these cases, humans have even caused the failure of their societies and a permanent disruption of the natural ecosystem. We could say that human habitation has been generally sustainable where there has been a long process of coadaptation between the human population and the biological community.

Migrations, on the other hand, have often been the cause of severe environmental damage, in so far as the populations that settle outside their traditional habitat not only exert an added pressure on the available resources, but they usually lack the institutions and the social practices that are required for a sustainable interaction with their new ecosystem. When the first human settlers arrived at the American continent 13,000 years ago for example, they were largely responsible for the extinction of the local megafauna, while in Africa, where humans and large mammals had evolved together, both populations could remain more or less stable. After some time, all human groups are able to develop the knowledge base, institutions and practices best suited to their new environment, but the arrival of new waves of immigrants may unsettle the whole system once again. Similar effects are often produced by the adoption of new technologies or foreign social institutions, especially when the group that adopts them has not yet been able to acquire compensatory practices. Much more problematic for sustainability are the structural dynamics linked to the habits or the foundations of human social systems. Perhaps the most relevant of these dynamics is the so-called tragedy of the commons, which illustrates how the exploitation of unowned or collectively-owned resources by rational individuals may inevitably lead to overexploitation, given that the individual optimum (to consume as much as possible) is incompatible with the collective optimum (to consume only what can be renewed). The ongoing processes of overfishing, air pollution and global warming are rather dramatic evidence that the tragedy of the commons is not just a theoretical model, but has very real effects. Of course, we should not rush to the conclusion that all natural resources need to be privatised. In the context of a market economy, the owners of these resources have strong incentives to exploit them in an unsustainable manner, especially when capital is mobile and the biological returns are lower than the financial returns of alternative investments. Other intrinsic mechanisms of the social system, such as cultural traditions, division of labour, competition between individuals or group rivalry, may also generate independent dynamics that ignore or aggravate environmental risks. The devastation of the natural ecosystem of Eastern Island, motivated at least in part by the elite's competition for status by means of erecting the Moai, is perhaps the most graphic and symbolic example. Great urban civilisations are particularly vulnerable to this kind of runaway cycle, where social complexity generates growing demands on the ecosystem on which cities depend, while their inhabitants are able to isolate themselves from the negative feedback loops that could curb the spiral of environmental degradation. Throughout history, therefore, every complex society has found itself trapped in a cycle of decreasing marginal returns, usually worsened by the systematic depletion of natural and productive resources which has often pushed it to the brink of collapse.

It would be insane, of course, to dismiss these lessons from the past or resort to the usual (and usually mistaken) argument that "this time it will be different". Our global civilisation is so faithfully following the patterns of expansion and collapse of the great historical civilisations that we are well justified in our concerns, especially if we consider that this time environmental collapse will affect all the ecosystems of the planet, while the scarcity of basic natural resources will have devastating effects on every human society. No matter how confident we might feel about our science and our technology, the truth is that we are ignorant of the real possibilities and limits of the earth's ecosystems. Nobody can tell us with any degree of certainty if we are still far away from collapse or we have already crossed the point of no return. In the light of the many signs of exhaustion, however, it would be wise to adopt the principle of prudence, a sort of Pascalian wager that would measure the relative insignificance of the sacrifices required to protect us against the immensity of the dangers derived from disregarding the signs of alarm. If we act on a mistaken assumption, we will lose very little. But if we fail to act, we could lose practically everything. Even the most sceptical anti-Malthusian should thus recognise the need to modify the mechanisms of our social systems in order to effectively promote forms of sustainable habitation and to deactivate the positive feedback loops that are driving the overexploitation of resources and the depletion of natural ecosystems. Collapse is not inevitable; sustainability and resilience have been properties of human habitation throughout history. We only need to ensure that our social systems take into account both the natural limits of the different habitats and the cultural traditions of the populations that inhabit them.

5 Inhabitants or Dwellers

The human subject, in spite of many philosophers' theories and the image often held by the subjects themselves, is not an entity that would precede in some way the thoughts with which it contemplates itself, the objects that it seizes, or the actions that it undertakes every time that it interacts with the world. This "subject without attributes", the supposed substrate of all qualities and experiences, is nothing more than a fiction created by the psychological mechanisms and sustained by the ideology of humanism. In reality, human beings cannot be understood apart from their existence, as if they were some kind of disembodied and unearthly spirits, capable of floating in the world of ideas before abruptly assuming the attributes of a particular life. Humans are, before anything else, beings-in-the-world. Not just "beings with a world"

45

or "beings within the world", but the constitution itself of being and the world in a concrete, material and temporal existence. Clearly, humans are not the only beings-in-the-world. We cannot even attribute to ourselves a special ontological richness that would separate us from the other animals. Like every member of the biological community, we inhabit the earth. Not because we occupy it physically, as if we could have occupied any other space and any other time, but because we are an integral part of this world, the product of evolutionary and adaptive processes that bind us seamlessly to all living beings. Our existence, shaped by specific habits and linked to specific forms of habitation, more than an attribute of our being, it is the essence. We are inhabitants and we cannot cease to be inhabitants without ceasing to be.

Earlier I defined "habit" as an individual's or a group's way of being, due to the confluence of genetically and socially acquired dispositions. I also defined "habitation" as the set of strategies, practices and institutions that allows the adaptation of a group to a given natural environment or habitat. In the same way, we could define "inhabitants" as the individuals who share habits and habitation. Leaving aside mental experiments, an individual inhabitant is a plain impossibility, considering that any form of habitation, human or non-human, is inevitably collective. We can, of course, speak of individual inhabitants, but we should always be aware that the existence of the inhabitant implies necessarily the previous, or at least the simultaneous existence of the group. Individual inhabitants cannot be confused with the group of inhabitants, nor can they be abstracted from the collective without immediately losing their meaning. At a certain level, all human beings are inhabitants, since they share habits and cohabit the earth. For a similar reason, all living beings are inhabitants, although it is quite obvious that the different species share habits and habitat to a variable degree. Applying the concept in another direction, but with the same logic, we can use the term inhabitant to designate those human or non-human beings that share certain habits and certain forms of habitation, excluding other human or non-human beings that do not share these same habits or forms of habitation to the same extent. The notion of inhabitant, like the ecosystem, is thus flexible and should be adjusted in every case according to the degree of speciation and to the actual context of habitation.

But what does it mean exactly to be an inhabitant? Which conditions define it and how does it interrelate with the other inhabitants with which it shares the world? In order to deal with these important questions we need first to understand the emergence of another figure, the citizen, which constitutes a kind of political avatar of the disembodied and unearthly subject so treasured by philosophers. As the main pillar of all discourses and legal constructions that sustain modern democratic systems, the citizen has always been, not a reality, but an ideal. If we accept as inevitable a certain discontinuity between ideas and facts, between words and things, the fictional character of the citizen would not appear to be particularly distressing. Citizenship, like law, justice or democracy, would be a watchword, a collective ideal that cannot be realised, but guides us towards a better world and protects us from falling into the abysses of the always feared state of nature. Yet, this function of guardianship of civilisation should immediately awaken our critical senses, especially when we see that politicians and theorists are only able to respond to the legitimacy crisis of current political systems by reinforcing this fiction and hoping that citizens, well educated in the virtues of citizenship, will meekly walk back into the fold of representative democracy. History shows, however, that political fictions, particularly when they are so far removed from reality that they become pure formal abstractions, have never sustained any building for too long.

The ideal of citizenship, as every Western citizen well knows, has its origin in ancient Greece, particularly in the 5th and 4th century Athens. The analysis made by two of its most renowned contemporaries, Plato and Aristotle, has weighed heavily on the whole political development of the West, from the Roman republic all the way to the modern nation-state; so much so that even today the word citizen draws its legitimacy and its effectiveness from the high hopes invested on it by the early Greeks. According to this ideal, citizens are members of a community, the *polis*, which they themselves rule. Certainly, Greeks restricted the status of citizen (*polites*) to a minority of the population, excluding women, children, slaves, foreigners, and very often even the poor. Many of these exclusions have been corrected later on due to changes in the mentality or the material conditions of society, while some others, such as the exclusion of foreigners and children, are still very much in place. Rather than the actual political system of the Greeks, however, what has inspired successive generations is the idea of a government of the community where all its members have the capacity both to be ruled and to rule. It is perhaps Aristotle who has delved more deeply into this idea and has contributed more decisively to perpetuate it up to the present day.

Aristotle begins from the premise that "a human being is by nature a political animal" (*zoon politikon*), a being who needs to live in community with other similar beings in order to realise its natural potential. The *polis* is just one of the possible organisations of society, but it is also the most perfect one, in so far as it allows human beings to live "as a community (*koinonia*) whose end is a complete and self-sufficient life". But how does it come about, according to Aristotle, that this common life ends up benefiting everyone and not just a few? "Things of this sort", he says, "are the result of friendship (*philia*), given that the deliberate choice of living together constitutes friendship". This concept of *philia* is crucial to understand the meaning that Aristotle gives to the *politeia*, which is not merely a legal or administrative commonwealth, not even a contract that would establish beforehand the rules of engagement between individuals in order to protect them from each other, but a voluntary and ongoing relationship of reciprocity between the members of the community. The *polis*, he claims, is the "community of the free" (*koinonia ton eleutheron*). By this, Aristotle is not just referring to formal or passive freedom, the freedom to do as one wishes without any restriction, but rather to the *polites*' capacity to participate in the collective decisions of the *polis*. It is the active participation in the life of the community, "the capacity to rule and be ruled" (*to dinasthai arkhein kai arkhesthai*), which constitutes in a proper sense the virtue of its members.

If the Greek citizen (*polites*) has traditionally served to define the ideal, the reality of Western political and constitutional history has been mostly influenced by a very different kind of citizen: the Roman *civis*. The notion of Roman citizenship emerged after a long process of development, closely linked with the military and territorial expansion of Rome. By the end of the republican period, in spite of some resistance from the nostalgic and the enlightened, citizenship was already an instrument of foremost importance in the great game of alliances and conquests with which the Roman elite had been submitting the different peoples and cities of the Mediterranean world. In this context, the notions of friendship (*philia*) and capacity (*dynamis*) that Aristotle had used to describe the citizen of the *polis* could not be much more than ideals without any practical effect. With the expansion of Rome, the ties of reciprocity between citizens tended naturally to weaken and political participation, which the republican *civis* could still hope to exercise indirectly through the *comitia*, gave way to the crude reality of imperial power. The citizen thus became a legal entity, a subject of rights and duties, but without any effective ties with the other citizens and without any capacity to participate in the government of the community. The notion of community itself was largely excluded from the Roman *civitas*, as shown by the fact that many of these new citizens, especially in the rich cities of Asia, kept a dual allegiance both as *polites* of their *polis* and *cives* of Rome. No Greek would have perceived this as a contradiction, as one was a political commitment while the other was no more than a legal subjection, whereby the citizen acquired certain duties (taxes) and some rights (judicial guarantees). Not surprisingly, Roman propagandists made every effort to give some political legitimacy to this sort of citizenship, relying most notably on the Stoic notion of cosmopolitanism. "The universe is a city (*polis*)", Epictetus and his followers had claimed, "you are a citizen of the universe". But these proclamations did not reverberate beyond a few minorities, at least until Christianity exploited them for its own ends.

Throughout Western history, this dual notion of citizenship, both a legal and a political status, has always hung in a precarious balance. More often than not, as in the medieval *bourgs*, the Roman conception of the *civis* has served to articulate society in view of promoting economic cooperation and organising the relations of property (bourgeoisie), whereas the Greek notion of the *polites* has had, when taken into account at all, a purely ideological function as an ideal aspiration or a propagandistic motif. In general, though, the burgeoning civil society of the Middle Ages was mostly founded on the feudal elaboration of Roman legal concepts, such as fidelity or patriotism, which exalted the service and attachment to the "city of the father" (*patria*). At the same time, the notion of sovereignty, as developed by Jean Bodin and others, tied the exercise of political power (the capacity to rule) to the hierarchical structure of society. Within this framework, formalised during the Renaissance, the king occupied the apex of the social pyramid and exercised his power by divine right, or as a direct descendant of Adam, according to the peculiar doctrine with which some tried to underpin a building that was already showing evident signs of ruin.

Born from the revolt against absolute monarchy, modern liberalism did not however renounce its implicit concept of sovereignty, in so far as the priority was not to undermine the mechanisms of power, but to displace those obsolete forms that still hindered the full development of private economic activity.

Liberal theorists such as Locke, adopting some of the principles of natural law, stated quite clearly that "the great and chief end of men's uniting into commonwealths, and putting themselves under government, is the preservation of their property". The state appears thus as the providential outcome of an explicit or implicit contract between free individuals who renounce part of their freedom in exchange for security. In this context, the active participation of the citizen in the political decisions of the commonwealth is only an accessory element of citizenship, useful up to a certain point in order to ensure its legitimacy and stability, but not so much as to warrant any form of democracy that may interfere in the private activity of the *homo economicus* or put his property at risk. There is no doubt that these preventions guided the Founding Fathers when they drafted the American constitution and established a political system that combined democratic elements (elections, checks and balances) with aristocratic or oligarchic elements (representation, bicameral legislature, restriction of the franchise). Modern citizens were thus defined in the tradition of the Roman *civis*, as mere subjects of rights and duties, despite the usual republican rhetoric and the limited powers granted to them under the system of representation. As the Supreme Court declared many years later, citizenship is not much more than "the right to have rights".

At the same time that the liberal regimes evolved under the legalistic and passive framework of the *civis*, the ideal of active participation inspired by the Greek *polites* continued to exercise an almost fatal attraction, undermining the stability so coveted by the bourgeoisie. "The English nation", wrote Rousseau, "thinks that it is free, but is greatly mistaken, for it is so only during the election of members of Parliament; as soon as they are elected, it is enslaved and counts for nothing". But the ideal of participatory citizenship was in fact incompatible with the scale of the large European states, as Rousseau, who had his native Geneva and other Swiss cantons in mind, was well aware. "With regard to the best constitution of a state", he claimed, "there are limits to its possible size so that it may be neither too large to enable it to be well-governed, nor too small to enable it to maintain itself by itself". This optimal dimension of the state was thus based, as in the case of Aristotle, on the relations of reciprocity between the members of the community. Even someone so drenched in Platonism as Rousseau would have earnestly denied that a large state like France could ever adopt a constitution such as the one he was proposing. And yet his ideals, mixed with other doctrines that proclaimed the malleability of human beings and the indefinite progress of humankind, contributed decisively to the successive attempts to bring the ideal into reality, from 1789 to 1917, with the results that everyone knows well enough. It would be a mistake to conclude, however, that the ideal of a "community of the free", as Aristotle had defined it, is simply unattainable and that we should just content ourselves with clearly bounded mechanisms of political participation. If the ideal of the *polites* has generally failed in modern societies, it is not due to an absolute impossibility, but to the absurd attempt to carry it through under certain political conditions (the nation-state) and under certain ideological postulates (the doctrines of progress and the blank slate), which turn the Aristotelian notions, otherwise quite sensible, into dangerous delusions.

Should we embrace, then, the liberal notion of citizenship as the best solution of compromise, considering that it alone seems able to articulate the increasingly large, complex and diverse societies of our time? Somewhat simplified, this is the argument that is usually put forward in order to justify the current political model where a passive citizenship is ruled by elites organised in competitive factions or parties. And it might have been a compelling argument if the myth of citizenship had not become so detached from reality that it is not longer able to sustain the legitimacy and the stability of the whole system of representative democracy. If the liberal citizen has nearly become a chimera, it is not due to the pressure of the ideal, but rather to the internal dynamics of liberalism itself. Certainly, Western democracies have continued to enlarge the regime of citizen rights (civil rights, political rights, social rights). They have not done so out of altruism, of course, but often pushed by internal and external pressures, or driven by the need to manage the population more effectively and give an adequate response to the challenges of technological change and economic globalisation. This process shows the flexibility and adaptability of the system, but only a chronic optimist could describe it as an "advancement of democracy". The truth is that none of these changes has served to increase the political capacity of Western citizens, only to expand the boundaries of their legal rights. Even the franchise of previously discriminated groups has not modified in substance the regime of participation of the citizens in political life. Indeed, in many cases it has served to restrict its efficacy even more. This rigidity of representative democracy explains better than anything else why the extension of social rights, while contributing to the general growth of the economy through an increase in the disposable income of households, has had such a modest effect on the reduction of real inequalities in many liberal societies. Of course, the restriction of citizens' participation in modern democratic systems is not just a clever tactic of the rich and the powerful to remain in power and retain their privileges; there are actually good reasons that explain it. The constant expansion of the world's economy during the past few centuries has led to the formation of increasingly larger political commonwealths: first the nation-state, and now the confederations of states such as the European Union. These political units respond to the need to attain a certain scale of the market, a certain efficiency of production, and a certain military capacity to preserve or expand all of it. Caught in the midst of this process of enlargement, the democratic aspirations of Western citizens are inevitably frustrated. Even if they have acquired new rights, they are still *cives*, not *polites*. And yet, the same political system needs to uphold the ideal of democratic participation of citizens as a source of legitimacy, in a process that tends naturally towards cognitive dissonance. As it was already the case in ancient Rome, the growing abyss between an actual legal status and a fictive political status has to be bridged through propaganda. Thus, the political capacity of the citizen becomes the motif of all rhetoric at the same time that the real citizens are increasingly confined to the mere exercise of the so-called "civic virtues".

One of the most evident symptoms of this sickness is the phenomenon of "political distrust", which political scientists associate with the decreasing levels of voter turnout in advanced democracies, with the general decrease in party affiliation and with the growing mistrust towards politicians of all signs. As shown quite clearly by the opinion polls, the problem is not that citizens are turning away from politics in general, much less from the principles of democracy, but rather from the norms, procedures and institutions of a political regime (representative democracy) that rhetorically exalts their capacity at the same time that it drastically curtails their real potential. In spite of the politicians' interest in minimising this problem, the truth is that the current system of representation, generally configured like a mechanism of contention, tends to turn citizens into consumers and politicians into producers. Politicians produce discourses that citizens consume, not by going to the supermarket once a week, but by going to the ballots once every four years or so. In this sense, the citizen of a modern democracy has as much power as the buyer of yoghurt; he can choose the brand, but not much else.

The comparison between citizens and consumers, widely used by political scientists and by the political parties themselves as they design their marketing strategies, is not just a fancy analogy. The citizen is, in effect, the equivalent at the political level of the consumer at the economic level. In the context of a globalised society, both of them have become abstract figures, individuals without attributes whose only essence is a legal or a virtual status that makes them perfectly interchangeable and submits them quite easily to the regime of statistics. The subsequent segmentation of this population of undifferentiated voters or consumers, through the attribution of particular preferences and characteristics, facilitates the task of their management and ensures an optimal allocation of the offer and the demand, whether of products or discourses. The active participation of the citizen or the consumer in this strongly technocratic structure is seen as unnecessary, even counterproductive, as it may disrupt the process of distribution of physical and social goods and reduce the global productivity of the system. Thanks to the mechanism of market allocation, citizens or consumers are thus able to see their preferences fulfilled, but always within the strict limits set by the operational requirements of social reproduction. In order for the whole machinery to work, however, citizens and consumers must be kept under the illusion that they are the ones who are actually making the decisions and leading the course of society, an ideological effect that advertisement performs quite admirably.

In the case of citizens, therefore, the distance between fiction and reality has not ceased to grow. Politicians' calls for an active citizenship are at best invitations to exert some form of local or sectoral activism, when they are not rhetoric concessions to the myth of citizenship that serves to legitimise modern democratic systems. In practice, the citizens of the nation-state, particularly of the large states, are subject to the rights and obligations defined in the laws of the commonwealth, but their capacity to intervene in the political process that leads to the formation of these laws (the capacity to rule) is extraordinarily limited and generally restrained by intermediary institutions such as the political parties, which more than channelling their participation, manage it under the pressure of special interests. In spite of the sometimes ludicrous arguments of political scientists, there is no denying that this incapacitation of citizens in most Western democracies is the main reason why they are becoming increasingly distrustful. The political system, organised by the party structure and the media on the basis of elitist principles, which are rarely recognised in public, does not expect too much from citizens' participation, except when the elections approach and it needs to "win" their vote. But if the political system does not expect much from citizens, why should we be so puzzled that citizens are no longer expecting much from the political system?

Unlike citizens, inhabitants are embodied beings, embedded in a natural and a cultural environment, members of a human community but also of a biological community. Habit and habitation define the inhabitants. They are not just features of their supposedly self-standing essence, but constitute their being-in-the-world. From the moment they are born in a certain environment, sons and daughters of certain parents, surrounded by a certain culture and heirs to a certain history, inhabitants acquire certain habits and share a certain project of habitation. The acquisition of habits is, in particular, a very complex process that often involves the interaction of genetic and cultural factors. Language is perhaps the most prominent example. It seems quite likely that all humans are born with a kind of universal grammar, a hard-wired psycholinguistic model that allows them to learn rapidly, especially during their early age, any language that they hear spoken around them. Almost all children, as is well known, learn the language of their parents. When this language is different from the language of the environment, however, children tend to learn the language or the linguistic variety of the environment, rather than the one spoken by their parents (or at least, both of them, but with a clear preference for the language dominant in the social environment). This explains why children of immigrants acquire easily and without any foreign accent the habitual language of their host country. And with language, they acquire all the other social habits, regardless of the dominant culture in the family. From this point of view, the child of an immigrant family and the child of a native family share in principle the same social habits and forms of habitation. They are, therefore, inhabitants to the same extent. This is also true of adopted children, especially when they have been adopted at a young age and are able to acquire the habits of their new social environment. Regardless of their origin, genetic differences between human individuals are so small that innate factors cannot warrant any distinction between native, immigrant or adopted inhabitants, as long as all of them have been exposed to the same social habits. The children of immigrants naturally share the dominant habits of their social environment and are thus able to blend into a community from which their parents still feel somewhat estranged. Of course, inhabitants can always move from a particular habitat to another habitat and live a perfectly fulfilling life in their new environment. But migrants, shaped by a slightly different set of habits, will always miss their original habitat, no matter how much they value the advantages of migration. Homesickness is, fundamentally, a lack of habit.

Both the habits and the forms of habitation affect the relationship of inhabitants with their environment, with their community and with their culture. But there is nothing deterministic in any of these relationships. Individuals are certainly capable of modifying them to a certain extent. As emigrants change habitation, they will acquire new habits, even if they may never be able to modify some of them. The liberal vision of the person as a subject who precedes his own ends is certainly a false one, but it does reflect a real capacity of individuals to alter some of their conditions and to pursue ends that may not be shared by the whole group. From this psychological adaptability, however, one cannot conclude that humans are by nature, as Kant and others have claimed, free and rational beings, "moral persons" who are able to judge autonomously and independently the conditions of their existence and to choose freely their own vital options. At least in this respect, the communitarian critique of liberal idealism is perfectly sound. But even communitarians tend to speak of individuals as previously existing entities, ghosts in the machine that may have not created themselves in the Kantian sense, but are still able to pursue a path of self-discovery and self-identification, which seems to fulfil the circle of personality. In reality, inhabitants are always already their own habits and do not need any cognitive effort or moral journey to find themselves. Habits are not, however, fixed and invariable foundations, but rather a kind of unstable terrain, a sandy shore that fluctuates with the undercurrents of nature and culture, and on which the inhabitants build, temporarily, their home.

Communitarians also tend to forget or ignore the fact that many habits are shared by all human beings. This is what justifies, more than the idealist fiction of the moral personality, a universal conception of justice. Human habits are, as we have seen, both egoistic and altruistic, both self-minded and cooperative. In any community, even in one based on common genetics such as a family, the ties that bind their members are basically those of strong reciprocity. Not just the hope of a reciprocation of favours in a determinate or indeterminate future, but the natural tendency to cooperate with other members of the group in order to achieve common objectives and to give each other mutual support in case of adversity. This behaviour of humans in every society is neither a rational assessment of benefits and costs nor an irrational outburst of feeling, but a way of being, a habit shaped by genetic and cultural factors that cannot be isolated in order to find the underlying "moral person", because they constitute morality itself, embodied and embedded in the inhabitant. This moral habit, like many other habits, is never exercised blindly. Rather, it is always dependent on the actual circumstances of habitation, on the characteristics of the environment, on the social institutions and on the behaviour of the other inhabitants. The feeding habit, to use a plain example, is shared by all animals, who would in the right physiological and environmental circumstances dedicate a significant part of their activity to put it into practice. Under the threat of a predator or a rival, however, this habit is rapidly inhibited and the animal puts into practice other habits that are equally effective, such as escaping or fighting. Similarly, the cooperative habit of humans, more than being a permanent and unconditional disposition, responds to contextual factors such as the availability and accessibility of resources, the cooperative disposition of other individuals, previous experiences of cooperation with these same individuals, the existence of cooperative institutions, and so on. As shown by social experiments and ethnographic observation, inhabitants are indeed capable of adjusting their level of cooperation according to the other inhabitants' attitudes and habits. If some of them behave in a selfish way, hindering common action or seeking individual benefits from cooperation without contributing their part, many inhabitants will react with indignation and will modify their behaviour, either refusing to cooperate or punishing the free-riders. Indignation is thus the habitual reaction of humans to the unilateral breach of reciprocity. Or to put it differently, indignation is the natural response to injustice.

Leaving aside its Kantian underpinnings, John Rawls' theory of justice is perhaps the most successful attempt to articulate the intuitions and habitual practices of humans in the context of social cooperation. Rawls develops his conception of "justice as fairness" in order to establish the constitutional foundations of a well-ordered society. This is a society, as he says, "in which (1) everyone accepts and knows that the others accept the same principles of justice, and (2) the basic social institutions generally satisfy and are generally known to satisfy these principles". He then suggests a hypothetical situation where different individuals, ignorant of their natural capacities, their social condition and any other factor that may influence the benefits and costs of cooperation, have to establish the principles that should regulate society. According to Rawls, "the persons in the initial situation would choose two rather different principles: the first requires equality in the assignment of basic rights and duties, while the second holds that social and economic inequalities, for example inequalities of wealth and authority, are just only if they result in compensating benefits for everyone, and in particular for the least advantaged members of society". Rawls' theory articulates very convincingly these two principles, the "principle of liberty" and the "principle of difference", on the basis of the individual rights and obligations of persons, who are thus able to pursue their own life project. At the same time, these individuals are effectively constrained by the obligations derived from the fact that they are part of society and benefit, in one way or another, from social cooperation. This idea of justice is egalitarian, as Rawls says, because "no one gains or loses from his arbitrary place in the distribution of natural assets or his initial position in society without giving or receiving compensating advantages in return". The difference principle would therefore express "a conception of reciprocity".

The artefact of the original position, like other elaborations of the social contract theory, is a legitimate way of articulating the idea of justice as long as we avoid giving it, as Rawls too often does, an explanatory value. Humans are not "free and rational persons"; they can neither make their way through life independently of their natural and social conditions, nor sit around a table to decide in an autonomous and unconditional manner the principles that should rule society. The fiction of moral personality may help us to expound the principles of justice already exercised in reality by the inhabitants, in so far as they have genetically and socially acquired certain cooperative habits that allow them to evolve in actual contexts of habitation. But to think that humans exist somehow outside society and nature, in the neutral space of ideal rationality, is simply absurd. Communities are not associations of free and rational individuals, as the doctrine of the social contract tends to assume, even when it does not postulate an explicit or historical celebration of such a contract.

Rather, communities precede and determine to a very large extent the rational and emotive decisions of individuals. The autonomous and independent person is merely a philosophical abstraction. No community has ever been formed by the union of such persons, because such persons do not exist anywhere beyond our concepts. We, humans, are always already inhabitants, members of some form of community, often of many communities at the same time (biological, cultural), whether we have been born into them or we have joined them later in life. Inhabitants, therefore, cannot decide to change community like they change their hat. The community has at least shaped part of their habits and if they were to change habitation, or even to acquire new habits, the community that they have "left" would still be part of them beyond the effective ties of cohabitation. In this sense, the liberal vision of a "community of humankind", founded on the fiction of the autonomous and transcendental subject, is no more than an idealisation, the universal projection of our own moral longings. Like the community of the Olympians, it has its abode where the winds never shake it, the rains never drench it, nor does snow ever fall upon it.

Communitarians are wrong, however, when they claim that the embeddedness of individuals in community invalidates in some way the universality of the principles of justice. The values, institutions and cultural practices of the different human communities are not, as social constructivism claims, independent evolutions of a perfectly malleable human nature, and therefore incommensurable. Many human habits are shared by all members of the species, basically because we all have a common genetic constitution. Amongst these human universals there are selfish dispositions, but also selfless ones. Individual autonomy and collective cooperation are not values that can be bartered at the flea market of cultural relativism, but fundamental habits of the human species, whose infraction universally raises a claim of outrage and indignation. The concrete expression of these habits depends to a large extent on the cultural and natural context, on the conditions of habitation and on other historical or contingent factors. But individual autonomy and collective cooperation are in themselves transcultural habits, largely conditioned by innate dispositions that have been selected genetically through a long process of common evolution. There is no need to rely, therefore, on the fiction of a moral and rational personality in order to justify the existence of universal moral principles. These principles are universally valid because they correspond to the social nature, genetically and culturally conditioned, of the *zoon politikon*. The infraction of these habits is thus morally indefensible, not because we are applying cultural value judgements, as multiculturalism claims, but because we apply principles of justice that are universally binding.

While the principles are universal, their concrete application is conditioned by the specific context of habitation. The ties themselves, therefore, are not universal. Humans are not bound together in the same degree, but according to effective (although not necessarily affective) relationships of reciprocity and friendship. The principles of justice, in other terms, are never applied abstractly between "moral persons", but between inhabitants, individuals who share habits and forms of habitation. In the context of the theory of justice, liberals are certainly right when they defend the value of individual autonomy against the impositions of the group (principle of liberty). But this autonomy, even in a strictly individualistic sense, is never absolute. Rawls himself is forced to restrict the list of freedoms (basically the civic and political ones) that should be included in his first principle of justice, in order to avoid a conception of liberty too large to be productive. His principle of difference, on the other hand, introduces some important restrictions on the substantive freedom of individuals, in so far as it limits their autonomy in the social and economic spheres in order to strengthen the ties of reciprocity. While this seems to complete the project of egalitarian liberalism, we have not yet resolved the question raised by communitarianism. If individuals are not, in reality, the free and rational persons depicted by liberal theory, but are rather constituted by their social and cultural embeddedness in a particular community, how can we integrate the ends of the community in the principles of justice without jeopardising the essential guarantees of individual autonomy?

We could extend this argument to include not just the human community, but the whole of the biological community. In general, communitarians do not take this step, which would imply giving moral consideration to non-human animals and perhaps even to the rest of living organisms, an idea that finds stiff resistance from the anthropocentric prejudice still prevalent in most contemporary societies. Rawls himself, while acknowledging the ethical obligations of humans towards nature and other forms of life, denies that the principles of justice could be extended beyond the human community, in so far as only humans are supposed to be free and autonomous subjects, capable of recognising each other as moral equals. But this idealist conception, as we have already seen, ignores the realities of habitation and the existential embeddedness of the beings-in-the-world, whether human or non-human. Furthermore, it is increasingly difficult to sustain a moral theory that sets its boundaries across the species divide, in the same way that no credible moral theory could sustain these boundaries with regards to race, gender or mental capacity. The progressive extension of moral consideration to other animals, beginning with the sentient ones (those who have the capacity to feel pleasure and pain), but eventually also to the rest of organisms, shows quite clearly the need to find ways of incorporating the other living beings, even species and ecosystems, to the community of justice. While it is not yet a major trend even amongst ecologists, there is a growing number of people who recognise that this incorporation could be perfectly achieved within the limits of liberal democracy, with no need to renounce the values of individual autonomy and social reciprocity. Ecological justice, more than just dealing with the distribution of natural resources between human populations, is concerned with extending the notions of distributive justice to include as well the needs and the legitimate aspirations of all the other organisms that cohabit with human beings. It is not yet clear, however, under which constitutional arrangements this extension of the principles of justice to the biological community could be effectively achieved. Most proposals continue to be attached to the abstract notion of moral personality that underpins the whole theory of ethics, even when they recognise the complexity of the ties that bind living beings to their natural habitat. The question raised by ecological justice is, nonetheless, extraordinarily important for any definition of justice that aims to free itself from the straitjacket of anthropocentrism. How can we integrate the needs and ends of the biological community in the principles of justice without jeopardising the needs and ends of the human community?

In spite of obvious theoretical and practical difficulties, it is possible to give an answer to both the communitarian and the ecological concerns without renouncing the liberal principles of justice. In order to do that, however, we need to include within these principles the reality of habitation, the fact that individuals share habits and are part of a community of inhabitants. This means that the principles of justice, as defined in the original position, cannot be limited to liberty and difference (or rather, fairness), but should also include a principle of care. It is perfectly possible to justify such a principle within the framework of the social contract theory, as the outcome of a universally accepted agreement between an undetermined community of participants, irrespective of the conditions and substantive vital options of its members. Rather than floating in the abstract sphere of unearthly moral persons, however, the principle of care takes into account the actual context of habitation and the effective relationships between inhabitants. By extending the fundamental principles of justice to include the habit of friendship (care), besides individual autonomy (liberty) and reciprocity (fairness), we will thus be able to bring together into the community of justice the present, past and future inhabitants (communitarian condition), but also the human and non-human inhabitants (ecological condition).

Later on, I will develop these ecoliberal principles of justice in some detail. At this stage, we should just acknowledge that it is the notion of the inhabitant, as opposed to the abstract citizen, that allows us to move beyond the morass of prevailing political theories.

As mentioned earlier, the double articulation of citizenship, both as a reality (*civis*) and as a fiction (*polites*), has become in a certain way the keystone of the great cathedral of contemporary democracy. The liberal project advances with determination, albeit not always consciously, to strengthen the legal status of citizens, while restricting at the same time their effective political capacity. Most liberals try to breach this gap by rhetorically exalting the virtues of citizenship, and will probably continue to do so for a while, at least until the democratic fiction becomes totally unnecessary for the full development of mercantile relationships. As for citizens themselves, it is increasingly clear that the current situation cannot be sustained for too long. The growing unrest in Western societies shows with particular urgency the need to reconsider in depth the foundations of our commonwealths. While we should not relinquish the liberal ideals of individual autonomy and a basic system of universal rights, it is crucial that we pursue once again the aspiration of living, as Aristotle said, in "a community of the free". It is not a matter of idealising the Greek *polis*, much less of projecting a utopia where peace and harmony will reign forever, but of stating in the strongest of terms that we are not going to renounce the ideals of the *politeia*, the active participation of all inhabitants in the context of a community based on the principles of justice, even if we have to develop new and richer forms of bringing it forth. Were we to renounce this historical task, the citizen of tomorrow, devoid of friendship and capacity, will not be much more than a legal fiction or a figure of speech.

6

Habitat
or the Nation

The nation is like the Hydra. A creature with only one body but so many heads that no one, not even its most heroic opponents, have yet been able to behead it. The simple mention of the word stirs all sorts of antagonistic passions, from the most unconditional of endorsements to the most angry of rejections. Nationalism is seen by many as a repulsive beast that should have been drowned in the marshes of history. And yet the nation, in its liberal or republican versions, still constitutes today the only framework of political legitimacy in advanced democracies. Even where the stench of bodies piled up in the name of the nation still lingers in the air, flags flutter, hymns trumpet, and citizens are asked to mobilise under such euphemistic slogans as constitutional patriotism or republican loyalty. An air of dissimulation and hypocrisy seems to surround all references to the nation and the national feeling, as if no one would want to be seen next to her, while everyone tries as best he can to win her favours. In this masquerade that has become Western politics, perhaps only the truly committed cosmopolitans, if there are actually any, preserve some degree of intellectual coherence, even if they then go on to bury their heads in the clouds.

If we really want to take on the challenge of creating a community of the free, as Aristotle defined it, we should assume the idea of the nation with all its consequences, without hiding behind half truths and empty calls to collective responsibility. The undeniable persistence of the nation throughout history reflects, whether we like it or not, the human need to live in politically meaningful communities, not just under a legal regime of rights and duties. The nation remains a valid concept because it has an adaptive value that goes well beyond a simple ideology or the fantasies of power-seeking elites. In principle, individual autonomy has no need for the nation and can thrive pretty well under a minimal state. But effective cooperation between individuals of the human species is unthinkable without the framework of a legitimate political community. The nation is one of the institutional expressions, historically conditioned, of this community. Of course, we should not accept just any kind of nation, particularly those that stand up in the name of an alleged community of blood or genes. But perhaps we should no longer accept either the nations of modernity, populated with such imaginary figures as the citizens or the sovereign people. Certainly, the legitimacy crisis of current nations will not be solved by appealing to "civic virtues" at the same time that the actual political capacity of citizens continues to be curtailed. But neither will the solution come by strengthening the mechanisms of participatory or deliberative democracy, if we have not been able first to give a solid foundation to the ties that should bind the members of the political community. The essential ecopolitical notions of habit, habitation and inhabitants, exposed in the previous chapters, attempt to set the grounds for a conception of the nation as habitat that may allow us to move beyond the liberal or republican nations, incorporating the needs and ends of the community, both human and biological, to the demands of individual liberty and social justice. This ecopolitical nation should thus be able to integrate the legitimate concerns of communitarianism and ecologism without renouncing the achievements of liberalism and social-democracy. Moreover, the model of the habitat-nation should be able to stand as a feasible alternative to the current model of the nation-state, which has evolved historically through the military, economic and political acquisition of various territories and by assimilating, often violently, heterogeneous populations. While the ideology of nationalism and the homogenising action of the state have been able to induce some degree of solidarity between the citizens of large nation-states, these bonds are usually too weak and too artificial to sustain forms of political participation that could overcome the limitations of the present systems of representative democracy. Without friendship, as Aristotle knew very well, there is no capacity.

From a broad perspective, the question "what is a nation?" is a particularly difficult one to answer. Contemporary political theorists tend to find two general responses: the primordialist and the modernist. According to primordialism, the nation would be a human community founded on ancestral bonds, cultural or genetic, which justify in some way its historical continuity and its projection towards the future. Modernism, on the other hand, defines the nation as a real or imagined community stemming from the social processes of Western modernisation and closely linked to this particular historical context. The distinction between both approaches is not as clear-cut as these basic definitions may suggest. There are many types of primordialism and many types of modernism. There are also many contributions that are hard to identify with one camp or the other. The current debate, in any case, is still very much dominated by modernists, who tend to depict primordialism in such crude terms that the modernist narrative seems almost inevitable. While I cannot enter into this debate in any detail here, there are some important critical points to be made regarding each one of these theories of the nation.

If the primordialist thesis implies that nations, as they exist today, are entities with immemorial or historically-deep origins, then it is obviously false. Nations, whatever they are, even if they have no substance at all, are the result of historical and largely contingent processes. Certainly, nations are often characterised by underlying factors which may have had a long permanence in time, such as the geographical or environmental substrate of habitation. There is no necessary link, however, between a particular national group (or any other form of political community) and a particular territory or habitat. The myths of autochthony, the stories that explain how current inhabitants arose from the land, are nothing more than fictions that attempt to legitimise certain ties with the environment of habitation. In truth, all human groups inhabiting a certain territory are the outcome of processes of cultural and biological adaptation to their environment, derived in every case from relatively recent migratory movements. This fact does not diminish in any way the relevance of the actual dependencies that link inhabitants to their habitat. Darwin's finches did not emerge by spontaneous generation from the different Galapagos Islands - they immigrated. But this fact does not make them any less adapted, nor less dependent on their habitat.

If the primordialist thesis implies that the political articulation of the community that we currently identify as a nation, although not necessarily the particular nations themselves, is immemorial or has deep historical origins, then it is not very accurate, but not completely false. As modernist critics have often remarked, the process of modernisation has given today's nations certain features that distinguish them from equivalent political forms of the past, such as the Jewish religion-nation, the Greek city-nation, the Roman republic or the Medieval city-state. The primordialist thesis has nonetheless a point of truth, in the sense that the modern nation, rather than beginning *ex nihilo*, has evolved from the previous forms of political and ideological articulation of the community. At this point, academic debates tend to degenerate into a pure terminological discussion, with the modernists defending the restrictive application of the term nation to the most recent phenomena and the primordialists (or rather, the perennialists) trying to expand it in order to cover the most ancient phenomena. Whatever we call them, there is no doubt that human communities, pre-modern or modern, have always striven to articulate themselves on the basis of shared habits and shared forms of habitation. The actual mechanisms of articulation of these political communities, shaped by a variety of environments, histories, cultures and genetics, are certainly very diverse. Even more diverse are the subjective representations that have been usually elaborated from these habits and forms of habitation, such as the symbolic identification of the different communities with particular territories, languages, religions or cultural practices. Beyond this diversity, however, the need to organise themselves in meaningful political communities is clearly universal, and thus primordial amongst human beings.

If the primordialist thesis implies, therefore, that the modern articulation of the political community that we call a nation, but not necessarily the particular nations themselves, stems from community dynamics that are immemorial or have deep historical origins, then it is fundamentally accurate. To be precise, this thesis is actually closer to the arguments of the so-called ethnosymbolists, who defend a certain continuity between modern nations and the social or cultural formations that preceded them. Unlike primordialists, however, ethnosymbolists tend to give too much weight to subjective cultural representations (myths, cults, memories, identities) and to ignore or undervalue the biological foundations of human behaviour, which are nonetheless essential to understand the persistence of ethnosymbolic communities. Of course, we will look in vain for an immutable essence that would be able to define any particular nation. There are nonetheless many habits, not only at the level of the national community, but at the level of every community, which tend to persist, culturally and genetically, across generations. These habits are not just attitudes that have been internalised by individuals during the process of socialisation, as the tunnelling vision of social constructivism would suggest, but the outcome of dialectic processes of interaction between inhabitants and their communities. Habits are always undergoing change, since they are basically cultural and biological adaptations, which evolve at variable rates and are largely dependent on the circumstances of the environment and the contingencies of history. At the same time, however, habits have a certain inertia, a tendency to persist in time, in so far as they contribute to the inhabitants' fitness and resilience (ultimate explanation) and are invested with value by the inhabitants themselves (proximate explanation). This inertia of habits explains the persistence of particular forms of habitation over long periods of time without the need to summon any immutable or transcendental essence that would magically bind together the individuals of the group. In the case of humans, characterised by a significant degree of exogamy and by their capacity for cultural accumulation, this inertia of habits is largely dependent on the mechanisms of social transmission of information. In consequence, the particular habits of human groups are never unavoidable; they do not stem from a common origin, nor are they necessarily projected into a shared destiny. Rather, they are the result of complex group dynamics and processes, such as fusion and fission, compromise and conflict, adaptation and failure. In the time span of a human life, or even a few generations, habits may seem more or less stable, in some cases even invariable. A wider perspective, however, shows that habits evolve and adapt to the circumstances of the natural and social environment. To claim that any human community shares a destiny because it shares habits is therefore plainly false. What ensures the persistence of a particular community of inhabitants is not the accumulated habits themselves, but the extent to which these habits are able to sustain their common habitation, their cohabitation, in the long term.

Modernist theories, on the other hand, attempt to explain the emergence of the nation and the ideology of nationalism as a consequence of political, economic or social processes of the last two or three hundred years. As long as these explanations recognise the existence of previous communities, their arguments are relatively innocuous for our discussion. It is perfectly reasonable, and to a certain extent justified, to establish a distinction between pre-modern and modern nations. The theories of modernism may be more or less accurate, more or less relevant, but in general they do not contradict the idea that all human groups have sought throughout history to articulate their political community according to their shared habits and forms of habitation. In fact, many of these modernist narratives strengthen, even without realising it, the argument that the recent emergence of nations and the discursive formation of nationalism, whether motivated by economic conflicts between the centre and the periphery, by the power struggles of the elites or by the need to homogenise industrial societies, has only been possible because the affected populations aspired to live in politically meaningful communities, many of which had to be articulated from previously existing social bonds. Before the sweep of modernity, communities may have had the size of a kingdom, a fief, a parish, a city or a tribe. But their existence, regardless of the role played by the elites and the extent to which they were integrated in larger units, responded to a fundamental need to articulate the realities of cohabitation in a politically legitimate manner. The degree of continuity between these pre-national communities and modern nations has to be analysed case by case, taking into account the specific historical and social processes, not only as they are reflected in the literary record, but also at the silent level of the effective human communities. Notwithstanding their relevance, these enquiries can never be conclusive. If the nation, in its manifold expressions, has become the privileged form of articulation of the political community in modern times, we will not gain anything by denying its validity or by denouncing it as a baseless invention. No matter how they have evolved historically, nations exist in so far as inhabitants have assumed them, voluntarily or not, in a more or less critical way, as the legitimate form of organising their cohabitation. The problem of the nation, therefore, more than just historical, is fundamentally political. And the question that we should be asking is not so much "what or when is a nation?", but rather "how do we want our nation to be?".

This is precisely what the model of the habitat-nation attempts to do by moving away from the traditional debates on the limits and possibilities of nations. It should be remarked from the beginning that the ecopolitical theory is not descriptive, but rather normative. More than just presenting an ideal-type, its aim is to describe the theoretical foundations of a political community that could be effectively realised and would be capable of responding to the needs and aspirations of its inhabitants. The habitat-nation should not just reflect the natural and social conditions of the present, but should also organise itself so that these conditions may be regenerated in the future, in order to sustain the human and biological communities in the long term. After all, nation and nature share the same Latin root, *natio*, which means birth, the constant regeneration of life out of the conditions of life itself. A complete community, as Aristotle stressed, "comes to be for the sake of living, but it remains in existence for the sake of living well". The Greek nation-state was nonetheless founded on the strict separation of the *oikos*, the domestic sphere of women, children, slaves and other properties, from the *polis*, the political sphere of free men. The habitat-nation, on the contrary, aims to reintegrate in the political community the whole of the *oikos*, not just the private habitat of the family, but the larger habitat shared by all inhabitants. Only by redefining the nation as an inclusive and shared habitat can we hope to overcome the narrow boundaries of humanism and leave behind the conception of the earth and the other living beings as resources for our unlimited appropriation. Many indigenous peoples, well aware of the interdependencies that bind them to all things, have developed forms of relationship with their habitat based on reciprocity and friendship. We, moderns, cannot go back in time and embrace once again primitive forms of habitation, such as the ones derived from hunting, gathering and horticulture, no matter how socially and ecologically sustainable they might have been. We can, however, find new ways of inhabiting the earth and re-establishing the bonds of friendship with all the other inhabitants, both human and non-human. The nation, conceived as a habitat, could perhaps become a hospitable home for this new community of free inhabitants.

We could begin by defining the habitat-nation, at least provisionally, as "the community of individuals who share a way of being, due to the confluence of genetically and socially acquired dispositions, as well as the set of strategies, practices and institutions that allow them to adapt to a given natural environment". This definition puts together the notions developed in the previous chapters:

(1) habit: an individual's or a group's way of being due to the confluence of genetically and socially acquired dispositions;

(2) habitation: set of strategies, practices and institutions that allow the adaptation of a group to a given natural environment or habitat;

(3) inhabitants: individuals who share habits and habitation.

More concisely, the habitat-nation may be thus defined as the community of inhabitants. This definition, however, is not precise enough, given that we have not yet established the geographical boundaries of the habitat. According to our premises, the community of inhabitants could be, amongst others, on the scale of an island, a valley, a city, a peninsula, a continent, or a whole planet. Nothing allows us to discriminate in advance on which of these scales, if not on all of them, a habitat-nation could be effectively developed. Before proceeding, therefore, it is necessary to determine somehow the geographical scale of habitation best suited for a given community of inhabitants.

A first approximation to this problem would naturally recommend the use of ecological arguments. After all, we are speaking of a generic community of inhabitants, without yet determining their species. It is thus in the science of ecology where we should be able to find the tools to circumscribe the scale of habitation. In general terms, though, a habitat is nothing more than the place where an organism lives, which may be defined at a very small scale (the territory) or a very

large one (the biome or even the biosphere). The
concept by itself does not give any indication as to the
biogeographical distribution of organisms. What is
more, biological communities are never distributed
within clearly outlined areas, but rather in ecosystems,
which are integrated at different levels and
interconnected through open and dynamic borders.
While it is possible to determine the boundaries of
these ecosystems, even to represent them in maps, this
implies necessarily a certain simplification and some
degree of arbitrariness. One of the most widely used
units in land-management, for instance, is the
ecoregion, which may be defined as a geographical set
of landscapes linked by ecological interdependencies.
Without entering into the technical details, it is quite
evident that the limits of an ecoregion can never be
determined with precision and will depend to a large
extent on the aims of the cartographer. Thus, the
World Wildlife Fund has identified a total of 867
terrestrial ecoregions in the world, defined as
"relatively large units of land containing a distinct
assemblage of natural communities and species". This
division, aimed at helping in worldwide conservancy
efforts, emphasises the distinctive character of the
biological communities and results in a substantially
different map from others that give more weight to the
interdependencies between the various communities
and the biophysical environment. In spite of its many
limitations, the ecoregion, as a geographical unit
defined exclusively by criteria of ecological integration,

is a good approximation to the scale that a meaningful community of inhabitants should attain, at least as long as we ignore the peculiar features of human habitation.

It is obvious, however, that we cannot ignore humans for too long, if only because practically all of the world's ecoregions have been profoundly altered by human habitation in the past few thousand years. The capacity of the species for cultural accumulation, on the other hand, prevents us from defining the boundaries of social communities exclusively in ecological terms, as we can do in principle with biological communities. If the habitat-nation has to include also humans, we cannot ignore the historical aspects of habitation and the cultural dimension of habits, without which the geographical delimitation of the habitat would be almost meaningless. We could say that the existence of an ecoregion is a necessary, but not a sufficient condition for the existence of a habitat-nation. To a certain extent, the definition of a geographical and political scale that would integrate the human and the biological communities in a meaningful way is the founding principle of bioregionalism. As a movement, however, bioregionalism has tended towards forms of re-inhabitation that stress the cultural or spiritual transformation of individuals, often under deep ecological tenets. This is probably due to the fact that bioregionalism has evolved in a cultural and ideological context, the United States, which is characterised by a fairly recent habitation of the land and by the absence of human communities effectively bound to their habitat. In this sense, the idealisation of the surviving indigenous peoples, while practically reducing them to indigence, is quite revealing. In spite of the wider postulates of bioregionalism, the concept of the bioregion, as a geographical unit defined in terms of the interdependencies between the biological community and the social community, is certainly a valid one. In principle, therefore, we can consider the bioregion to be the necessary and sufficient geographical scale for the development of the habitat-nation.

But the definition of the concept is not enough to establish with any precision the scale of the natural and social environment that should actually delimit the meaningful community of inhabitants. We need criteria that allow us to discriminate between potential scales, not in an abstract sense, but in every particular case. According to Aristotle, this criterion should be self-sufficiency (*autarchia*), the capacity to live with one's own resources without depending on the external world. The interconnectedness of ecosystems shows, however, that self-sufficiency is not a feasible ideal, given that bioregions are always dependent on other bioregions and all of them are dependent on the global system of the biosphere. Even if we were to restrict it to the sphere of society, the ideal of self-sufficiency implies a refusal to extend the bonds of cooperation between humans, for example through trade, which can only be upheld, and always precariously, through the means of coercion. In the present economic and technological context, self-sufficiency could only lead to large states, with autocratic governments and inequitable social structures, which would also tend to be harmful to the environment. Unlike the Greek city-nation, therefore, self-sufficiency cannot serve to determine the optimal dimension of the habitat-nation, even as a regulatory principle.

Another criterion that could allow us to determine this dimension is economic efficiency, that is, the degree in which the political community is able to achieve an optimal equilibrium between the benefits of scale (availability of public goods) and the costs of heterogeneity (impairment of the social and political system). From this point of view, the optimal dimension of states tends to decrease as the institutions are more democratic, there is more freedom of external trade, and there are supranational levels of integration which allow the most onerous public goods to be shared. These economic considerations, however, do not help us to determine with enough precision this optimal dimension, since they only provide a static picture and do not take into account the fact that political communities, like individuals, have a past and a future, and that this past and this future are interconnected in a dynamic present. In order to find the optimal equilibrium, therefore, we should take into account the capacity of the community to persist in the long term, not just to exist at a particular point in time. Another problem of these models is that they tend to ignore the externalities of the social system, both domestic externalities (the effects of the social community on the biological community with which it cohabits) and foreign externalities (the effects of a given social and biological community on all the rest). Clearly, these interdependencies are crucial to the survival and development of the ecopolitical community and must be considered when determining the optimal scale of the habitat-nation.

Beyond self-sufficiency and efficiency, therefore, the criterion that could allow us to define the most adequate scale of the habitat-nation is sustainability, that is, the capacity of the community to regenerate its own natural conditions. This criterion has two different dimensions: ecological sustainability (the regeneration of habits and forms of habitation by the biological community) and social sustainability (the regeneration of habits and forms of habitation by the social community). Sustainability is not just a matter of regenerating natural resources, but should also take into account the regeneration of all the economic, social and cultural aspects of the human community that sustain its habitation over time. Otherwise, we would arrive at the conclusion that sustainability can be determined at a global level (for instance, by a world government), ignoring the fact that habitats are sustained by the actual human and biological communities that inhabit them. If the biological community is not sustainable, neither will be the human habitation. And if human habitation is not sustainable, it will inevitably tend to disrupt the biological community. The optimal scale of the habitat-nation will be thus determined by the extent to which a social community and a biological community are able to cohabit in a sustainable manner by regenerating their own natural conditions with a minimum of negative externalities.

Before examining both aspects of sustainability in more detail, we can reformulate our definition of the habitat-nation in the following terms: "the community of individuals who share a way of being, due to the confluence of genetically and socially acquired dispositions, as well as the set of strategies, practices and institutions that allow them to adapt to a given natural environment in a sustainable manner". It is not yet a fully satisfactory definition, but it allows us to introduce the temporal dimension of the community, in so far as its persistence over time depends on the regeneration of the natural conditions (habits and habitation) that sustain it, both at an ecological and a social level.

When speaking of ecological sustainability, it is customary to use the expression "sustainable development", defined by the United Nations as meeting present needs without compromising the ability of future generations to meet their own needs. Many perceive this association of sustainability with development as quite an unsustainable oxymoron. And certainly, it would be better to speak of sustainable habitation, considering that economic development, whether good or bad, is just one of the aspects of human habitation. Sustainable habitation, moreover, cannot be restricted to the goodwill interventions of public administrations and citizens in the area of natural resources management. This is only a partial vision of sustainability, which ignores the fact that many communities have been sustainable in the past without the need for public policies, an organised state or theoretical conceptions of sustainability. Sustainable habitation is thus a practice of inhabitants, which stems from the genetically and culturally evolved habits that have allowed the successful adaptation of the different groups to their own habitat. In the specific case of humans, the habits that contribute to ecological sustainability, even if through very different means, are autonomy, reciprocity and friendship. Human inhabitants may sustain their natural environment for their own interest, motivated by the benefits that they can extract from it: this is the principle of exploitation of the habitat, which tends to perceive the biological community as a productive resource that should be maintained and regenerated, in so far as it is necessary for the development of human habitation. At the same time, human inhabitants may sustain their natural environment out of a sense of reciprocity, motivated by the interdependencies that bind them to the rest of the biological community:

this is the principle of cooperation with the habitat, which tends to preserve the services that ecosystems provide to human habitation and to limit the negative effects of this habitation on the function of ecosystems. Finally, human inhabitants may also sustain their natural environment out of a sense of friendship, motivated by the intrinsic value of the biological community to which they belong: this is the principle of care for the habitat, which tends to foster the conservation of the individual and specific members of the community, as well as the preservation of the conditions that allow them to regenerate themselves. All three aspects of sustainability are indispensable and should, in an ideal situation, balance each other. To exploit the biological community disregarding reciprocity and friendship would be so unsustainable as to impose some kind of deep ecological care of the environment that would ignore the reciprocal ties and the interests of human inhabitants. In general, however, it is not autonomy or reciprocity, but rather friendship, the philial element of sustainability, that is usually left behind in the process of structuring the political community. It is precisely this deficiency that inspired Aldo Leopold to stress the need for a new land ethic. "A thing is right", he pointed out, "when it tends to preserve the integrity, stability and beauty of the biotic community". Ecological sustainability implies, therefore, that the political community should adopt the principles of justice derived from autonomy, reciprocity and friendship, while ensuring their effective application to the whole of the biological community.

When speaking of the sustainability of a human community, we cannot just limit ourselves to the ecological conditions that make it possible. Relations between the members of society should also respond effectively to the principles of justice. To a certain extent, this requirement could be applied to all social animals, particularly to those who live in fairly complex communities. In many ways, these communities are already regulated by their own principles of justice, some of which humans are just beginning to understand. Of course, it would be absurd to suggest that the habitat-nation, structured on the principles and mechanisms of human justice, should also intervene in the internal regulation of other species' social communities. As long as the ecological conditions that allow them to develop according to their own habits are preserved, this aspect of sustainability may be regarded in practice as fulfilled. Obviously, we cannot adopt the same kind of detachment in relation to the social regulation of our own community. Not only because we have no other choice but to articulate in some way the cooperation between members of the species, but also because ecological sustainability depends to a large extent on the social sustainability of the human community (and vice-versa, of course). Social sustainability, on the other hand, cannot be restricted to the regeneration of individuals, but should also take into account the effective communities in which these individuals are embedded and which define, in a complex dialectical process, their particular habits. A community that would fail to distribute in a fair manner the benefits and costs of cooperation between its members would be as unsustainable as one that would fail to preserve and foster the habits that allow it to adapt to the environment of its habitation. Social sustainability, like ecological sustainability, is thus a practice that stems from these same habits, and in particular from autonomy, reciprocity and friendship. Inhabitants may sustain the human community for their own interest, motivated by the benefits that they can extract from it: this is the principle of exploitation of the inhabitants, which tends to perceive humans as productive resources that should be maintained and regenerated, in so far as they are necessary for the development of human habitation. At the same time, inhabitants may sustain the human community out of a sense of reciprocity, motivated by the interdependencies that bind them to the other members of the group: this is the principle of cooperation between inhabitants, which tends to ensure a fair distribution of the benefits of social and economic cooperation, while regulating the conflicts that may jeopardise an effective cohabitation. Finally, inhabitants may also sustain the human community out of a sense of friendship, motivated by the intrinsic value of other humans: this is the principle of care for the inhabitants, which tends to foster the physical, psychological and moral well-being of the individual members of the community, as well as the conditions that allow the community to regenerate itself. When conceiving and regulating social relationships, human communities, often organised by men, have always given much importance to autonomy and reciprocity, but have traditionally ignored or undervalued the public relevance of friendship, the philial element of sustainability, which has almost always been relegated to the domestic sphere of women. It is precisely this deficiency that inspired Carol Gilligan to stress the need for a new ethic of care. "This conception of morality as concerned with the activity of care", she pointed out, "centres moral development around the understanding of responsibility and relationships, just as the conception of morality as fairness ties moral development to the understanding of rights and rules". Once again, a well-organised social community must take into account both forms of morality. Social sustainability implies, therefore, that the political community should adopt the principles of justice derived from autonomy, reciprocity and friendship, while ensuring their effective application to the whole of the human community.

Sustainability will be thus achieved if the community is able to establish effective relations of justice between all inhabitants. Wherever a particular bioregion, that is, the geographical coincidence of a biological and a social community, is able to uphold these effective relations of justice, founded on the habits of autonomy, reciprocity and friendship, we can properly speak of a habitat-nation. This community will necessarily be a political one, given that it includes one species of *zoon politikon*, a kind of organism that regulates its society through the bonds of autonomy (individual interest), reciprocity (collective cooperation), and friendship (mutual support). In theory, a habitat-nation should thus include at least one group of inhabitants capable of articulating the principles of justice that are derived from these habits. In our planet, as far as we know, the only inhabitants with this capacity are humans. Accordingly, we may safely describe as political the community that includes human inhabitants and use indistinctly the notions of social and human community. We are not, however, excluding non-human inhabitants from the habitat-nation, just restricting it to those social and biological communities that are integrated, amongst others, by human animals and can therefore constitute themselves as political communities. We should also take into account, at least in principle, the possibility that two or more human communities may inhabit a common geographical area without sharing habits or forms of habitation in a sufficient degree to make up a single habitat-nation. There is no doubt that this situation presents some particular challenges for the ecopolitical community, or for any other form of community, but it does not preclude it altogether. However, I will concentrate here on those cases, much more common nowadays, where the political community is made up of the inhabitants of an exclusive habitat.

Being a political community, the habitat-nation faces the same problems as alternative theoretical models. Basically, there are two such models: the ethnic-nation and the civic-nation. This distinction, originally advanced in the context of modernist theories of the nation, has often been used by the nations themselves to gain some kind of absolution from the original sin of nationalism. Nationalists, from the point of view of the civic-nation, are always the "other". Its own nationalism is thus conveniently hidden or concealed by patriotic euphemisms that allow it to present itself as the common home of the citizens, supposedly defined in universal terms, without any form of ethnic or cultural distinctiveness. In reality, all nations have been built, or have attempted to build themselves, on the basis of a particular language, a particular religion, or some other particular feature of the dominant ethnic group. Taking into account that almost all pre-modern states were made up of a plurality of ethnic groups, this has been as much a process of "nation building" as "nation destroying". The suppression of the distinctive traits of minority ethnic groups within the so-called national territory through the mechanisms of assimilation or exclusion has been the norm rather than the oriental supplement of certain exacerbated nationalisms. Only when the nation-state has been culturally homogenised, or at least sufficiently unified under the essential elements of a distinct ethnic group, have the processes of civic legitimation of the nation been able to work their charm. National unity, presented as a fact of life, moves then to the background and becomes surreptitiously articulated through the mechanisms of banal nationalism, while the state goes about its civilising mission, both at home and abroad. Unfortunately for most nation-states, this comfortable balance is always threatened by the subsistence of national minorities or migratory processes, which may challenge the alleged homogeneity of the nation and unleash once again the assimilative or exclusionary violence of the dominant majority. The contrast between the ideal of the nation-state and the plurinational or pluriethnic reality of its population is particularly striking in the case of large states, built under the pressure of interstate competition during the process of modernisation. It is generally accepted that the modern system of nation-states was first articulated through the Peace of Westphalia (1648), which consecrated the principle of territoriality, with the definition of stable borders and an international balance of power between the dynastic states of western Europe and the empires of eastern Europe. In this new context, the large western states began to develop more active policies of cultural homogenisation, aimed at unifying their internal market, spreading a modern bureaucratic administration across their territory and ensuring their subjects' loyalty to the sovereign. The transition from the absolutist state to the national state, in the wake of the liberal revolutions of the 18th and 19th centuries, had little effect on the ultimate end of strengthening, both internally and externally, these same states. It was effectively established, however, that the legitimacy of this process did not lie on the monarch's, but on the people's sovereignty. In spite of the customary propaganda, this "people" was never a universal subject, lacking in ethnic identity, but always a particular nation, with a language, a religion or some other distinctive trait that could legitimise, according to the theory of the nation-state, the processes of internal homogenisation (national education) and external mobilisation (national army). Even then, conflicts continued to arise every time that an existing state attempted to assimilate all the inhabitants of its territory under a particular idea of the nation or when the inhabitants of a particular territory refused to be assimilated by the state and attempted to create their own nation-state. As is well known, these dynamics tend to feed each other, sometimes with disastrous consequences. The pretension of existing states to sanctify once and for all the present arrangement of sovereign nations is nonetheless indefensible. What justification could there be for the majority nations of a certain state to deny minority nations the same prerogatives of state-building that they have arrogated for themselves? The model of the civic-nation, with its notional community of abstract citizens, is often depicted as the solution to this problem. But as long as it remains tied to certain political units, the nation-states, justified by the existence of distinctive cultural or ethnic groups, it is hardly distinguishable from the model of the ethnic-nation that it is supposed to overcome. If it were coherent with its discourse, the civic-nation would resolutely advance towards the dissolution of the nation-states and the construction of plurinational or supranational political units such as the European Union. In that case, however, it would have to face a very serious problem of legitimacy and participation, as these very large units can never become meaningful political communities for their inhabitants. We should thus ask ourselves if it is possible to conceive some other form of nation, one which would avoid the homogenising and centralising patterns of the nation-state while allowing the inhabitants to actively participate in the democratic government of their community.

It should be clear by now that the habitat-nation is an attempt to model precisely this sort of political community. In order to appraise its theoretical relevance, we should ponder two different, but closely-related issues. One is the question of legitimacy: to what extent is the habitat-nation a more legitimate articulation of the political community than the alternative models of the nation? The second one is the question of cohesion: to what extent is the habitat-nation able to maintain a more cohesive political community than the alternative models of the nation?

Unlike the ethnic-nation, the habitat-nation does not draw its legitimacy from the previous existence of an ethnosymbolic community, whether real or imagined. This community, in so far as it contributes to the sustainability of cohabitation, may help to articulate the habitat-nation, but it is never indispensable. As happens in all human communities, some shared habits, such as a language, a religious cult or other relevant cultural practices, may indeed enter into a regime of ethnic distinction, whether these habits existed before the constitution of the habitat-nation or have resulted from subsequent processes of ethnogenesis. In any case, this community of habits does not determine the limits of the habitat-nation, as it does under the ideology of the nation-state. Even if a relatively homogeneous ethnic community inhabits a well-defined bioregion, those inhabitants do not just share habits at the bioregional level, but also at many other levels, both higher and lower. Habits are shared at the level of the family, the neighbourhood, the profession, the county, but also the region, the continent, and the whole planet. The definition of the habitat-nation does not give priority to any of these levels and does not postulate that the political community should be articulated on the basis of the habits that may distinguish a group from its neighbours. Inhabitants may share some particular habits, but the habits themselves are not what binds them into a meaningful community. Rather, it is the extent to which these habits are able to sustain their common habitation. Habits and habitation are the two indispensable terms of the equation that results in the habitat-nation. Without a shared habitation, the community of habits is largely irrelevant. Without some shared habits, the community of habitation is almost impossible. Once again, we should stress the fact that all humans share habits, given that they share a very similar genetic make-up, as well as many cultural traits. If habits were the only significant bonds between inhabitants, there could be habitat-nations formed by two friends or by the whole human population. Modern nationalism attempts to overcome this vagueness by selecting a few relevant habits, more or less objectively defined, in order to establish the boundaries of the ethnosymbolic group (a nation) that would legitimise the meaningful political community (a nation-state). Ecopolitical principles, on the contrary, rule out this form of ethnic legitimacy and ground the meaningful political community on the ecological and social sustainability of habitation. In short, the habitat-nation is the political community that allows the inhabitants to sustain their cohabitation over time. Of course, there is nothing in this definition that would deny a pre-existing ethnosymbolic group (a nation, in the usual terms) the capacity to constitute itself as a habitat-nation. In order to do so, however, the habits which are shared by its inhabitants and which differentiate them, subjectively or objectively, from other social groups, must not be the legitimising principle of the political community.

But if the habitat-nation does not find its reason for existence in the ethnic community, how can it pretend to overcome the lack of legitimacy of the civic-nation? Does it not find itself in the same situation as all those theories that postulate the existence of a political community on non-nationalistic grounds, but then, in practice, are not able to sustain themselves without resorting in one way or another to the ethnosymbolic legitimacy? Certainly, like any theoretical construct, the habitat-nation could be used as an excuse for ethnosymbolic projects of nation-building. Unlike the civic-nation, however, the habitat-nation does not postulate the abstract identification of individuals with a state (citizenship), but recognises and incorporates the natural conditions, habits and habitation, that already bind individuals in effective communities of inhabitants, even if they are not yet political. While their borders are always difficult to determine, these ecological and cultural regions precede the state and may in many cases justify its constitution. But here we must be very careful not to generalise. Each human community, in the context of its own biological community, should ascertain by itself whether the habits shared by its inhabitants, particularly those that fasten the ties of autonomy, reciprocity and friendship, allow them to sustain their common habitation, so that they may, if they choose to, constitute themselves as a habitat-nation. From that point forward, the concrete articulation of the political community will largely depend on the circumstances of each particular context. To give general recipes, without taking into account the specific needs and possibilities of each individual community, would contradict the essential principles of the ecopolitical theory.

The main problem of the civic-nation, however, is not so much its theoretical legitimacy, but rather its incapacity to ensure the effective cohesion of the social community on the basis of the abstract principles of citizenship. Surely, the fiction of moral personality, with its tendency to ignore the habits acquired in the community, as well as the networks of relationships that bind the inhabitants together, is one of the causes of the progressive erosion of interpersonal and political trust in modern liberal democracies. In contrast, the theory of the habitat-nation does not justify the universality of the principles of justice on an idealist conception of human beings as moral persons, but rather on habits shared by all human inhabitants as a result of a common evolutionary process. In this sense, in so far as the cohesion of the social community derives originally from the principles of justice, the link between justice and trust is not merely contingent, but necessary. Where the habits of autonomy (liberty), reciprocity (fairness) and friendship (care) are able to sustain an effective cohabitation, the community will be united. As these habits weaken, social cohesion can only be maintained by increasingly coercive means, a path that eventually leads to the totalitarian state, where liberty, fairness and care have practically ceased to function as the binding principles of the community. These habits of autonomy, reciprocity and friendship, as well as the social bonds that are derived from them, never arise in the abstract sphere of the disembodied and unearthly moral persons of liberal theory. Rather, they are shaped in the context of individuals embedded more or less intimately in a natural, social and cultural environment. Each one of these habits stems from a process of genetic and cultural adaptation which cannot be understood in strictly individual terms. Even autonomy, a habit more directly explained by innate factors than the other two, always develops within a particular social context and could not be expressed outside this context. The myth of the lone wolf tends to forget the extraordinarily social nature of the wolf. In general, therefore, the cohesion of the group depends on the extent to which the habits of autonomy, reciprocity and friendship are able to bind the individuals into an effective community. These habits are universal, but the bonds they generate are always particular. The degree of particularity and the scale of the community are certainly variable. A family, for instance, is bound together by the habits of autonomy, reciprocity and friendship by virtue of a real or imagined genetic community. The evolution of these ties on the basis of inclusive fitness may be able to provide an ultimate explanation of the fact that family members are usually so attached to each other. The efficacy of this family bond is so obvious that almost every human community, whatever its size, has tried to legitimise itself and to promote internal cohesion by posing as a real or metaphoric family. Tribes proclaim themselves extended families, nations extol the fatherland, the mother country or the blood community, members of a religious order address each other as brothers, and so on. According to some theories, these bonds, at least in the case of ethnic groups, are not just a form of rhetoric, but actually correspond to an effective genetic relationship. The nation would thus constitute a real or putative *fratria*. Beyond very specific cases, like isolated tribes with a marked degree of endogamy, this thesis is difficult to sustain, as it tends to forget the complex process of genetic and cultural coevolution that has given rise to all human groups. But it is not in the sphere of reality where the idea of a national *fratria* has traditionally played its very significant role. The expansion of the modern nation under the revolutionary slogan of "liberty, equality, fraternity" shows quite clearly the symbolic relevance of family ties in justifying and promoting national cohesion. Self-proclaimed civic-nations have nonetheless maintained an uncomfortable relationship with the principle of fraternity. On the one hand, following their premises, they should have repudiated it, as it postulates a bond between citizens that goes well beyond the relationship of the individual with the state and is grounded on a real or imagined community of ascendancy. On the other hand, though, the need to unite the nation, not only for political or military purposes, but also in order to sustain social cooperation within the group, has justified its adoption in terms more or less sanitised from genetic or phenotypical connotations. According to its declared principles, republican fraternity is supposed to be colour-blind, in the sense that it treats equally all moral persons. As in Orwell's farm, however, some persons are more equal than others. It is a well known fact that fraternity, whether republican or liberal, has never stopped, indeed has actually encouraged the citizens from every nation to exterminate each other in the name of their own motherland.

Unlike the civic-nation, the habitat-nation does not deny the existence and the importance of ethnic groups, nor does it minimise the relevance of shared habits in the formation and sustainability of human communities. Effective social cooperation, whether stemming from reciprocity or friendship, requires a certain community of habits. Moral persons, if they actually existed, would not be able to form an effective community. At the same time, however, shared habits are rarely enough to make a neat distinction between one particular human group and another. Ethnicity defines the group as an "us" distinct from "them". This distinction is typically grounded on certain habits, such as language, manners or traits of character, which may be reconstructed or reinterpreted according to variable social contexts. Even where it is less substantial, as in the artificially-marked groups of certain experiments, there can be no doubt of its efficacy in generating trust and sustaining cooperation within the particular group. Indeed, it is a characteristic of the political animal to form symbolically marked groups and to organise social cooperation on the basis of existing bonds of reciprocity and friendship. The habitat-nation does not ignore this reality, but it does not turn it either into the founding principle of the political community. Ethnicity, as the self-identification of a particular social community on the basis of shared habits, may help to sustain human habitation and may also be beneficial for the biological community as a whole. As long as it supports the extension of the principles of justice to all inhabitants, both human and non-human, ethnicity may thus contribute positively to the sustainability of the habitat-nation, but it is never an indispensable element of this sustainability. The habitat-nation could also be articulated from pluriethnic communities as long as the habits and forms of habitation shared by the inhabitants are able to sustain both the social community and the biological community. Likewise, the existence of a particular ethnic community does not mean that it should necessarily constitute itself as a single political community. According to ecopolitical principles, it could well organise itself as two or more distinct habitat-nations. In some cases, for instance when the geographic extension of the ethnic community undermines the sustainability of cohabitation, such a solution might even be unavoidable. The habitat-nation is therefore not an *ethnos*, nor is it a *demos* or a *civitas*. What is it then that binds the ecopolitical community to the common objective of sustainability? "Things of this sort", as Aristotle said, "are the result of friendship (*philia*), given that the deliberate choice of living together constitutes friendship".

Instead of the foundational *fratria* of the ethnic-nation or the instrumental *fratria* of the civic-nation, the internal cohesion of the ecopolitical community is based on the *philia*; not on fraternity, but on friendship. At best, political theory tends to read Aristotle's notion of friendship as an affective supplement to reciprocity. More often than not, however, even reciprocity is disregarded by the so-called models of rational decision as a secondary effect of individual interest, the only motivation that would seem to befit human rationality. Consequently, liberal theorists prefer to obviate the question of friendship, as if Aristotle had been misled in this by a feminine sentimentalism, quite out of keeping for a rationalistic and serious philosopher. Even communitarians, in principle so sensitive to the ties that bind together human communities beyond individual autonomy, tend to confuse friendship with sympathy, love or some other form of affection. According to this interpretation, the logic of rights and justice appears necessarily opposed to the logic of affections and emotional relationships, even when the latter are being vindicated as valuable aspects of the community's political organisation. Once again, the model for this kind of thinking is the private sphere of the family, which liberals tend to leave outside the public sphere of justice, as it seems to be regulated almost completely by affections between relatives and is generally considered to be a natural union of interests, which therefore does not require a regulation based on law. Some have even suggested, for example in the context of Marxism, that the whole of society should function according to this idealised model of the family, a community founded, not on abstract rights, but on the particular affections of its members. Even those who accept the need for public principles of justice and a legal regime of rights and duties are quick to regret the absence of nobler virtues in public life, like love or friendship, which they associate with the private life of individuals. In reality, the family is also a regime of rights and duties, even if quite an informal one. At the same time, it is a community founded, like all human communities, on the habits of autonomy, reciprocity and friendship. In the case of the family, the bonds derived from these habits are certainly stronger than in most other communities, but they are not fundamentally different. To claim that society should function as a family, in the sense of incorporating a supposed fraternity that would be lacking in the larger community, is simply to ignore the importance of friendship in both the family and society.

Friendship is neither a mere expression of feeling nor a rational calculation of costs and benefits. When Aristotle speaks of friendship, he describes it as a *proairesis*, a term that could be translated as conscious or deliberate choice. It implies, therefore, a form of rationality, but not necessarily in the propositional or computational manner of the *logos*. Friends are chosen deliberately, although not in an abstract way, but rather in the context of personal relations within pre-existing and effective communities. Ethnographic observations and recent experiments have shown that individuals are better disposed to cooperate and to share with those whom they identify as friends, well beyond what one would expect if they were only motivated by interest and a sense of reciprocity. Friendship is thus a habit, a way of being that is expressed in the form of affection, love, attention, preoccupation, help, care and trust towards certain individuals, clearly distinguished from the others. Needless to say, there are varied degrees of friendship. Humans are perfectly capable of establishing qualitative and quantitative distinctions in the relations of friendship that bind them to individuals in their different social contexts. The degree of friendship binding a mother and daughter, for example, is not the same as the one binding the same mother to her friends at the bridge club or her daughter to her best friend at school. Friendship is a matter of relative proximity, whether real or perceived, between particular individuals. And it is precisely this proximity that justifies, through the psychological mechanisms of affection and trust, the significant levels of cooperation and support that are common between friends. Our disposition to help friends does not depend on the benefit that we may be able to extract from them, not even on our hope to receive some kind of reciprocation from them in the future. Rather, it is justified by the intrinsic value that we attach to each particular person. A friend is someone whom we value for him or herself and to whom we wish well. Far from being limited to the closest of relationships, the differential bonds of friendship spread through real or imagined interpersonal networks to the whole of society (*sociophilia*), even to the whole of humanity (*philanthropy*). Of course, individuals will not hold the same ties of friendship with people in their family, their town, their country, or the whole world. As in the example of the mother and her daughter, we all incorporate these interpersonal networks within an asymmetric structure of identifications, which take into account the real or imagined proximity to other individuals, as well as other more or less contingent factors. This extension of the ties of friendship beyond effective personal relationships is hardly surprising if we consider that friendship is the result of the same process of genetic and cultural coevolution that has given rise to human sociability and therefore constitutes a universal human habit, even if its expression may vary according to the specific conditions of each social group and individual.

Consequently, there is no reason to confine the habit of friendship to the sphere of private relationships, ignoring the fact that public life, without a certain degree of friendship between the members of the community, would be unsustainable. Friendship, as Aristotle remarked, "holds city-nations together", in so far as it is "the highest form of justice". Thus, friendship is not an affective supplement of justice, but one of its vital foundations.

The universality of friendship amongst humans, in spite of the variability of its cultural expressions, indicates that it is a peculiar habit of our species. There is some evidence that this habit may also characterise some other social species, such as the great apes and the dolphins, even if it is hard to determine it conclusively. In any case, there is no doubt that humans are able to extend their ties of friendship, not just to other humans, but also to non-human individuals. The mother and the daughter of the previous example may share their home with a dog, with whom they keep a relationship that can only be qualified, at least from their part, as a form of friendship. After all, we refer to the dog as the best friend of humankind for good reason. Even if they might not openly recognise it, many pet "owners" would rather sacrifice themselves for the well-being of their non-human friends than for many of their neighbours and acquaintances. Moreover, as with humans, this capacity to extend the bond of friendship beyond the species is not limited to those animals that share our household, but may also include other living beings that we do not have a direct relationship with. These animals can also enter, in one way or another, into the networks of identification that constitute the asymmetric circles of the *philia*. Our concern for some species threatened with extinction, the monetary contribution to a shelter that takes care of animals we will never meet or the affection we may feel for the animals appearing in nature documentaries are just some examples of the habitual tendency of humans to identify themselves and establish bonds of friendship with other living beings, even with the processes and natural environments that allow them to exist. The entomologist Edward Wilson has called this relationship *biophilia* and has argued that it is perhaps an innate tendency of humans, acquired by the species in the course of its evolution. Even if this hypothesis turned out to be incorrect, it is obvious that the habit of friendship, to the extent that it includes non-human organisms and processes as objects of care, also constitutes the basis for a form of justice that goes beyond the narrow circle of the human community.

We should not forget, however, the dark side of friendship. In the same way that we identify our friends, we identify our enemies, or at least those that are kept outside our asymmetric circles of friendship. Friendship's particularism has often been criticised as a perversion of the universal principles of justice, which should apply without distinction, it is argued, to the whole of humanity. But this circumscription of justice to humans is already a form of particularism, even if so widespread that it often seems unnecessary to give any ethical justification to it. The denial of the human habit of friendship or its confinement to the sphere of private life leads, in any case, to the construction of political communities based on abstract principles that are unable to ensure the effective cohesion of individuals around a sustainable common project of habitation. Even when theoretical principles ignore it, however, friendship is already weaving its knots through society and constitutes, beyond the formal regime of rights and duties, the real foundation of public life. Why then should we continue to withhold from it the "right of citizenship"? Why not incorporate friendship once again, as Aristotle wished, to the principles of justice, as an essential element of the political community beside autonomy and reciprocity?

The habitat-nation, legitimised and bound together by the sustainability of cohabitation, aims to integrate all inhabitants in the political community, not as brothers and sisters, nor as moral persons, but as friends. The deliberate choice of living together or cohabiting, and thus of sustaining each other and sustaining the common habitat, can only be the result of friendship. And only friendship, in so far as it extends the principles of justice to the individuals of all species, may allow the constitution of a community of free inhabitants.

After these discussions, we are now ready to suggest a definition, perhaps definitive, of the ecopolitical community:

"The habitat-nation is the community of individuals (inhabitants) who share a way of being, due to the confluence of genetically and socially acquired dispositions (habits), as well as the set of strategies, practices and institutions (forms of habitation) that allow them to adapt to (inhabit) a given natural environment (habitat) in a sustainable manner, thanks to the bonds of autonomy, reciprocity and friendship".

7   Ecoliberal Principles of Justice

The constitutional foundations of the habitat-nation are the principles of justice. A useful way to give a rational justification to these principles is by starting from the original position elaborated by John Rawls. We will need however to introduce some very specific modifications to his theory, in order to take into account the conditions of cohabitation and to discard any anthropocentric particularism in the constitutional structure of the well-ordered society. It is important to remark that neither of these modifications breaches the main assumptions of the social contract, even if we may end up with a slightly different constitution than the one most often defended by egalitarian liberalism. In so far as the essential elements of the liberal project are nonetheless preserved, this constitution could be accurately qualified as ecoliberal.

In his theory of justice, Rawls begins by setting up a sort of mental experiment: if a representative group of individuals could meet to decide the principles that should regulate society without knowing their individual characteristics and the position that they would have to occupy in this society, which principles would they choose? The intuitive idea of "justice as fairness", as Rawls suggests, is that a person who has to divide a cake without knowing which piece he is going to end up getting naturally tends to make a fair division of the cake. Commentators of the theory, sometimes even Rawls himself, tend to drift unnoticeably from an instrumental to a substantial interpretation of the original position. If we were to interpret Rawls' proposal in substantial terms, as a contract between virtual persons, the veil of ignorance that surrounds the parties would certainly be problematic. The definition a priori of the individual motivations that are kept inside or left outside the veil is quite arbitrary and weighs heavily on the outcome of the deliberations. From our point of view, however, only an instrumental interpretation is actually justified. We should thus see the original position, following Rawls, not as an imaginary situation articulated from the potential conditions of the parties, but as "an expository device which sums up the meaning of these conditions and helps us to extract their consequences".

Of course, being a mental experiment, there is no need to accept the conditions imposed in advance by Rawls, as long as there are reasonable arguments to discard or modify them. In this sense, the description of the parties in the original position as individual humans, unrelated to any social or biological community, not even an indeterminate one, has very little plausibility. "It seems reasonable to suppose", Rawls argues, "that the parties in the original position are equal. That is, all have the same rights in the procedure for choosing principles; each can make proposals, submit reasons for their acceptance, and so on. Obviously the purpose of these conditions is to represent equality between human beings as moral persons, as creatures having a conception of their good and capable of a sense of justice". If the original position were a virtual meeting between individuals who then go on to effectively live in the society they have themselves designed, Rawls' arguments would be fairly reasonable. But if the original position, as he himself indicates, is nothing but an expository device, there is no convincing reason to establish a priori that the parties should be human beings. In the context of a hypothetical interplanetary justice, for instance, the original position could not justifiably exclude the possibility that there would be other non-terrestrial species with a conception of their good and a sense of justice comparable, if not superior, to that of humans. The parties in the original position must of course be able to deliberate on the basis of a shared rationality, but this does not imply, unless we interpret the original position in substantial terms, that these deliberations could not take into account the interspecific distribution of goods and bads in the actual social and biological community which results from the contract between the parties. It would make much more sense therefore to conceive the original position as a hypothetical meeting of indeterminate individuals who know that they will inhabit the political community resulting from their contract, but are unaware of their natural, social or specific characteristics within this community. The shared rationality and equality in the negotiations are postulated as regulatory principles of this hypothetical original position, without prejudging in any way whether the parties will end up being humans, starlings or martians.

The interspecific equality in the original position's deliberations does not necessarily imply, however, an actual equality in the political community derived from the contract between the parties. It is reasonable to suppose that the parties in the original position, aware of the differences in habits between biological species, will structure the political community in such a way that the principles of justice may effectively discriminate between the different kinds of inhabitants. The intuitive idea is that freedom of expression, to give an example, may be a substantive element of liberty for a human being, but not for a starling. At the same time, the right not to be subject to torture is as substantive for a human as for a starling, although it has no sense for an amoeba. The parties in the original position could therefore agree on the basis of a rational argument accepted by all, whatever their subsequent speciation in the world may be, that the principles of justice should be applied according to a system of reasonable discrimination based on certain constitutional orders. These orders should not be seen, however, as a scale of values with ontological foundations such as the Medieval great chain of being. Rather, they are strictly founded on the habitual characteristics of the different types of organisms. It is from the habits, as well as from the capacities and interests derived from them, that we may be able to establish a differential constitutional arrangement, without giving precedence to any particular biological configuration. It seems reasonable to suppose that the parties in the original position will identify:

(1)   a political order, characterised by the habit of friendship, which capacitates organisms to organise themselves in complex societies based on mutual support and grants them broad interests in the spheres of society, politics, culture, religion, art, and so on;

(2)   a social order, characterised by the habit of reciprocity, which capacitates organisms to organise themselves in social groups and

grants them limited interests in the sphere of social interaction;

(3)   an individual order, characterised by the habit of autonomy, which capacitates organisms to be subjects of a life and grants them interests in their psychological and physical well-being, including those derived from family bonds;

(4)   a vital order, characterised by the habit of life, which capacitates organisms to live and gives them basic interests in their survival.

A well-organised political community should thus take into account the habitual differences that distinguish these orders when designing and elaborating its constitution. This does not mean establishing specific principles of justice for every order, but making sure that the political community develops and applies the universal principles of justice discriminating between each one of the orders that constitute it. It is important to remark in this sense that orders do not classify inhabitants, but rather habits. Humans inhabitants, for instance, would be included in the political, social, individual and vital orders. Elephants, on the other hand, would be excluded from the political order, but included in the social, individual and vital ones. In the same way, starlings would be part of the individual and vital orders, while amoebas would only be included in the vital order. After exposing the principles of justice, I will suggest some practical ways to apply this principle of reasonable discrimination in an actual constitutional context. For now it is enough to recognise that these orders, or a similar classification, could be perfectly acceptable as an interspecific foundation of the political community, without the need to abandon the expository device of the social contract.

Another essential element of Rawls' theory, and of liberal conceptions of justice in general, is the rejection of perfectionism, or rather the rejection of the idea that a public theory of justice should incorporate in one way or another the moral aspirations, whether individual or collective, of the members of the political community. This neutrality of the liberal state is not so easily sustained in practice, as many of the critics of liberalism, but also some of its advocates, have frequently pointed out. As a regulatory principle in the original position, we can nonetheless accept its validity, as long as it is coherently applied and does not serve to slip a certain vision of human society under the door. Rawls presents the question in terms of a distinction between the good and the right. Justice as fairness, he claims, would not attempt to maximise the good of the community, as utilitarianism does, neither would it promote, in the line of the different forms of perfectionism, a partial vision of the common good. As a deontological theory, it seeks to determine, based on a rational discussion, the general principles that should regulate the political community, allowing its members to choose for themselves the personal or collective goods that they value the most. The liberal theory of justice does not neglect to pursue the common good, but it stops short of incorporating it in any substantive manner in the determination of its principles. But how are the parties in the original position supposed to choose what is right if they do not have at least some idea of what is good? Rawls attempts to avert this vicious circle by slipping under the veil of ignorance what he calls "primary goods", that is, "things which it is supposed a rational man wants whatever else he wants". Needless to say, the selection of some primary goods or other will weigh heavily on the content of the principles of justice. We must therefore be very careful in the theoretical justification of this selection. According to Rawls, the primary goods consist basically of natural goods (health, vigour, intelligence, imagination) and social goods (rights, liberties, opportunities, income, wealth, respect). This list is justified, as Rawls himself points out, by a certain conception of human nature and social interdependencies. Even if we limit ourselves to human individuals, however, it is quite evident that the list is too partial and does not adequately reflect the most basic human needs and motivations. Rawls claims that his conception of the primary goods "is a familiar one going back to Aristotle". But what happened to friendship, which Aristotle described as "an absolute necessity in life"? In view of the partiality of Rawls' list, we should break loose from his theory at this point and suggest a more balanced and exhaustive conception of the primary goods, one which would also take into account that the biological species of the parties in the original position must remain outside the veil of ignorance. As a consequence, the primary goods cannot be determined from a certain a priori conception of human nature, regardless of its philosophical pedigree; they must be derived from our empirical knowledge of the behaviour, the needs and the interests of living organisms. In this sense, the basic habits that have allowed us to define the different constitutional orders will also provide us with the list of the primary goods. The four primary goods would thus be: friendship, reciprocity, autonomy, and life. All the primary goods suggested by Rawls are included in this list (autonomy depends at least in part on health and wealth, respect depends on reciprocity and friendship, and so on). At the same time, our list is more complete and less arbitrary than the one proposed by Rawls. It also has the advantage of potentially including all inhabitants, without prejudging or restricting the particular goods that individuals may pursue in reality, within the limits of their species, their social group or their inclination. In short, this list conforms more strictly to the neutrality in relation to the good that supposedly inspires the liberal theory of justice.

The neglect of friendship in Rawls' theory is clearly not so innocent as it might seem at first glance. To accept that friendship is a primary good would imply accepting that the community, and not just the individual, must somehow enter into the articulation of the principles of justice. It is around this question that the debate between liberals and communitarians often turns, with communitarians defending the need to ground the political structure of the community on some definition of the common good, while liberals continue to stand by the alleged neutrality of the state in respect to the different common goods that civil society may freely adopt. The pluralism of modern societies seems to support the liberal argument, but it is also true, as some communitarians point out, that these societies could not grow and prosper without relying on some idea of the common good defined at the level of the public principles of justice. There is ample evidence to support the idea that political communities are unsustainable without a sufficient degree of social cohesion. This cohesion cannot be induced from above, through the promotion of the so-called civic virtues, so treasured by republican theorists, just as it does not grow spontaneously, like a sort of mana that would magically bind together the community as a superorganism. Empirical studies have shown that the level of political legitimacy in a particular society is strongly conditioned by the degree of interpersonal trust; or to put it another way, by the degree in which friendship binds individuals in the pursuit of a common good. In a dynamic society, it is not so much civic virtues, but precisely the habit of friendship that is reinforced by interpersonal associations. Under these conditions, instead of a civil society, it would be much better to speak of a philial society, founded on the practice of responsibility and mutual support between individuals who are bound together by the extended ties of friendship. Where these ties cannot be channelled through the formal institutions of society, they tend to create alternative structures of cooperation, often in conflict with a misbegotten political system. The ties of friendship are thus indispensable for the democratic health of the political community, but only from an idealist and fundamentally coercive perspective may one pretend to shape them according to the abstract notion of good citizenship. This form of republican perfectionism is rejected with good reason by liberal thought, which regards it as another attempt to manage society from the state. In this sense, the reluctance of liberals to incorporate friendship in the principles of justice may be easily understood, given that human communities, whether religious, political or social, have traditionally tended to suppress individual autonomy in order to promote partial visions of the common good, which are then justified in the name of supposedly superior principles, such as the divine word, national interest or the common will. Yet, the solution suggested by these theorists is clearly unsatisfactory, considering that the alleged neutrality of the liberal principles of justice in respect to the common good is incapable of sustaining on its own the political community and depends on forms of perfectionism that are kept outside the social contract, as an implicit or concealed, but not necessarily just, framework of cooperation.

But how should we integrate the common good in the public principles of justice without subjecting the autonomy of the individual to the will of the group? Is it actually possible to conceive a common good that all members of the community may be able to accept, to the extent that it is not derived from any partial interest? Liberals assert that common goods of this sort do not exist, while communitarians swear that they do exist, but are unable to present a single convincing example. Traditions, cultural practices, values or ethical principles, not to speak of religious doctrines, are always linked, no matter how neutral they may seem, to partial visions of the good, which not all members of the community share to the same degree. If we were to define the common good on the basis of habits shared by a particular political community, for instance a language, we would be ignoring the fact that there may be members of this community who do not speak the same language or who do not speak it as fluently as other members. In any case, we would be defending a biased vision of justice, favouring certain individuals and groups over others. From the point of view of the original position, all these definitions of the common good are unacceptable. But liberals are simply wrong when they claim that there is no common good that could enter into the public principles of justice without breaching the neutrality of the original position. The ecopolitical notion of habitation will provide us with precisely such a good.

Sustainability of cohabitation is a common good shared by all members of the community, regardless of their community and regardless of their place within the community. While this good could be overlooked in the conception of the original position as a meeting of moral persons, we have already mentioned that such an abstract definition, to the extent that it is only an expository device, is not really justifiable. If we accept, as seems inevitable, that the parties in the original position are conscious of their condition as inhabitants, even if they are not yet aware of the community or the place within the community that they will actually inhabit, it is clear that they would all agree to accept sustainability of cohabitation as one of the fundamental principles of justice. There is no member of the political community, irrespective of condition or inclination, who would not consider *prima facie* sustainability of cohabitation as an indisputable value. As we have already seen, common habitation, both in its social and ecological dimensions, is sustained in part by autonomy and in part by a sense of reciprocity between individuals. In this sense, Rawls' principles of justice, the principle of liberty and the principle of difference (or better, fairness), already contribute in some way to the common good of sustainability of cohabitation. But these two principles are clearly insufficient on their own to guarantee this sustainability, as they ignore all non-instrumental relations between inhabitants. Hence, it would be reasonable for the parties in the original position to agree on a third principle of justice, the principle of care, which would take into account that sustainable cohabitation is an aim shared by the whole community of inhabitants, beyond each individual's interest and beyond the distribution of resources amongst individuals. Just as the principle of liberty is founded on autonomy and the principle of fairness in reciprocity, this principle of care is founded on friendship, one of the primary goods acknowledged under the veil of ignorance. The habitat-nation is thus established on the recognition that care must be, besides liberty and fairness, one of the fundamental principles of justice.

Before suggesting a possible formulation of these principles, it is important to give some consideration to the question of intergenerational justice. If we were to exclude from the principles of justice, as Rawls does, any reference to the community, we would be unable to incorporate intergenerational justice without postulating it a priori in the original position or assuming that the parties somehow represent a "continuing line of claims", which would include at the same time all generations. Both solutions are clearly unsatisfactory and show the extent to which a strictly individualistic theory of justice must make contortions to embrace intuitive notions that are perfectly natural and sound when regarded in terms of community. Starting from the ecopolitical theory, we do not need to look very far to find a justification for the principle of solidarity between generations: sustainability of cohabitation, which the parties in the original position have accepted as a common good, is already such a principle. In addition to being articulated both in relation to the social and biological communities, sustainability must necessarily take into account, as a principle grounded on temporality, the relation of inhabitants to the present community (inhabitants must sustain the actual cohabitation), to the past community (inhabitants must sustain the habits and forms of habitation received from previous generations), and to the future community (inhabitants must sustain the habits and forms of habitation for the following generations). Sustainability of cohabitation is thus an intergenerational principle of justice, as well as an intragenerational one. Without a community of habits and habitation, this principle would be meaningless. It is the persistence of the political community, not as a superorganism or an invariable substance, but as the deliberate cohabitation of inhabitants, bound together by the ties of autonomy, reciprocity and friendship, that justifies the collective rights and duties of care, in the same way that it justifies the collective rights and duties of liberty and fairness. The common good of sustainability implies therefore that inhabitants should take care of the habits, practices, strategies and institutions inherited from previous generations, in so far as they help to sustain their common habitation. The common good of sustainability implies, furthermore, that inhabitants should take care of the habits, practices, strategies and institutions that they have acquired or invented, in so far as they might help to sustain the common habitation of future generations. Finally, the common good of sustainability implies that inhabitants should take care of the inhabitants themselves, in so far as cohabitation, more than a meeting ground for individual interests or a complex network of reciprocities, is the necessary context where the different individuals and species are able to pursue their own good; not just life, but the good life.

Now that we have justified their adoption, we are in a position to formulate the principles of justice that should ground the constitution of the habitat-nation:

> *Principle of liberty:* "Each inhabitant is to have an equal right to the most extensive total system of equal basic liberties compatible with a similar system of liberty for all other inhabitants".

Principle of fairness: "Inequalities in the access to economic, social or natural resources between inhabitants are to be arranged so that they are to the greatest benefit of the least advantaged".

Principle of care: "Inequalities in the access to vital opportunities between inhabitants are to be arranged so that they are to the greatest benefit of the community as a whole".

While the first two principles restate quite faithfully Rawls' principles of liberty and difference, in the case of the habitat-nation their application is not exclusively restricted to humans, but it includes all inhabitants. According to the premises of our original position, the parties would have previously agreed to segregate the political community in constitutional orders, on the basis of the habits that define the different capacities and interests of living organisms. The principles of justice are thus formulated in a universal manner (they refer to indeterminate "inhabitants"), but the constitutional and legislative arrangements of each habitat-nation could apply them unevenly to the different orders. At the level of justice, the articulation of these substantive universal principles with a regulatory principle of reasonable discrimination is sufficient to establish the fundamental framework of the ecopolitical community. Of course, this will not resolve all ethical or political questions in respect to the explicit or implicit claims of justice of the inhabitants, far from it. But the principles of justice, as Rawls points out, are not supposed to embrace the whole of ethics. The distribution of the specific rights and liberties will therefore lie on each political community, according to the system of government that the inhabitants have freely given themselves. A particular habitat-nation may decide, for instance, that all inhabitants, regardless of their order, have the same right to life and that killing any kind of organism is against the law (in practice, this would be a difficult society to live in, but it is theoretically possible). Another habitat-nation may decide that killing inhabitants of the individual order is illegal, but deny the same protection to the inhabitants of the vital order (in this case, the carnivorous diet would be outlawed). Finally, a third habitat-nation may decide that killing inhabitants of the political order is against the law, but deny the same protection to the other orders (this would be the current situation in most legal arrangements); even if it may grant them other rights (such as some degree of protection against torture in the case of the social and individual orders, and so on). Obviously, the development of the principles of justice in respect to non-human inhabitants will always be asymmetric, given the fact that only members of the political order are able to participate directly in the deliberation and formulation of the laws that should regulate the entire political community.

Members of the political order acquire thereby a superiority in might, but not in right, over all other inhabitants. The principles of justice cannot do anything to prevent human inhabitants from using their effective power to deny, for example, any kind of legal right to other organisms. In an ecopolitical community, however, human inhabitants must give some form of legal articulation to the principles of justice in relation to the different constitutional orders. The legislative devices adopted in practice by the community, such as allowing the representation by proxy of non-human inhabitants, as well as the specific rights granted to the different orders, are issues that should be settled in the course of each habitat-nation's political process. This lack of definition may seem unsatisfactory, but the current nation-state regulates itself in the same manner in respect to human rights. The generally accepted principles of justice recognise, for instance, the right to life of all humans, but then the legal arrangement of each nation is likely to establish exceptions, which may be more or less justified, such as the death penalty, abortion and other controversial cases. Similarly, the ecoliberal principles of justice do not determine a priori the effective legislation of the habitat-nation in respect to the rights of non-human (or human) organisms. The fact that the ecopolitical community must give an explicit and constitutional articulation to these principles in relation to the different orders is nonetheless a significant improvement from the present situation.

Another noteworthy departure from Rawls' theory is the introduction of the principle of care. This is justified, as we have seen, by the consideration that sustainability of cohabitation is a common good that the parties in the original position would want to include in the principles of justice, not just by virtue of the primary goods of autonomy and reciprocity, but also by virtue of the primary good of friendship. The principle of care reflects therefore the fact that inhabitants have an interest in sustaining their common habitation, not just for instrumental reasons or for a sense of reciprocity, but because they regard this cohabitation as valuable in itself, regardless of any direct or indirect benefits they may be able to obtain from it. Moreover, this principle incorporates, at least in part, the feminist criticism of the impersonal principles of justice most often upheld by liberal men. From the point of view of an ethic of care, justice should not be restricted to the regulation of the rights and duties applicable to abstract moral persons, disregarding the networks of interpersonal relationships that make up the effective community (and also, in most cases, also the affective community, but we should insist on the fact that friendship is not merely a matter of affections). Justice would thus have to attend both to objective claims (such as breached freedoms or the unfair distribution of resources) and to subjective claims (such as the physical or psychological suffering of individuals). This extension of the notion of justice should not undermine in any way the universality of its principles, which is not justified by an abstract conception of moral personality, but by the fact that all inhabitants share, albeit differentially, some basic habits such as life, autonomy, reciprocity and friendship. Once more, the application of the principles of justice is always particular, but the principles themselves are universal. The incorporation of care into the sphere of justice does not contradict this universality, even if effective care depends most of the time on the private interpersonal networks of each inhabitant. The principle of care does not attempt to regulate in any case these interpersonal networks, just as the other principles do not regulate each inhabitant's plan of life or the particular arrangements of reciprocity between inhabitants. These three principles establish a public conception of justice, which affects the constitutional configuration and the basic structure of society, not the private life of each individual or group. The introduction of care as one of these principles implies therefore that a well-organised political community should establish the necessary public mechanisms to implement it in practice under the terms defined in the original position. It is important to remark, once again, that justice does not embrace the whole of ethics. The principle of care does not include all forms of care that may be found in society, from mutual aid between friends to a mother's attention to her baby or her dog. Only those forms of care that may be publicly regulated and can be defined in acceptable terms for the parties in the original position should be governed by the principles of justice.

The principle of care suggested above states that "inequalities in the access to vital opportunities between inhabitants are to be arranged so that they are to the greatest benefit of the community as a whole". This notion of "vital opportunities" incorporates, in the first place, the habit of life that characterises all living beings by the mere fact of being. Life is, in this sense, an opportunity that can be realised by all biological organisms. In the case of the inhabitants of the vital order, survival exhausts the content of their vital opportunities. As we move through the different constitutional orders, however, the concept is enriched with those elements that characterise the good life for the different kinds of organisms: well-being (individual order), sociability (social order), and culture (political order). The access to the vital opportunities in the case of humans includes therefore the access to life, well-being, sociability and culture. Or in other words, these vital opportunities define the good life for humans.

An additional benefit of the notion of vital opportunities is that it allows us to give a substantive content to the principle of liberty, which Rawls leaves in a certain ambiguity, arguing that "it would serve no purpose to classify systematically the various liberties". According to our principles, inhabitants are free as long as they are able to realise their vital opportunities. In this sense, the first principle of justice would encompass liberty in negative terms (being free from the obstacles that might impede the realisation of one's vital opportunities), while the third principle would introduce a more positive notion of liberty (being free to effectively realise those opportunities). The aim of care is therefore to capacitate inhabitants so that they are able to realise their vital opportunities, more than just ensuring a legal or institutional framework that allows them to realise them by their own means.

Vital opportunities should not be confused, however, with social, economic or natural resources, whose distribution is regulated by the principle of fairness. According to this principle, inequalities in the access to resources cannot be justified on the basis of differences in natural or social endowments, but should respond to the effort and decisions of each inhabitant. At the same time, these inequalities should not be so large as to weaken the ties of reciprocity that make up a well-ordered political community. Differences in income between human inhabitants, for instance, would be justified if they contribute to improve the economic situation of the whole of society, and particularly of those who have been less favoured by the social or natural distribution of capabilities. This same principle could be extended, on the basis of reasonable discrimination according to the constitutional order, to non-human inhabitants, in order to implement for example interspecific policies of environmental or distributive justice. I will not go into any detail on this question here, nor will I discuss in depth my principle of fairness, which modifies to some extent Rawls' principle of difference. I should insist nonetheless on the fact that the principle of care does not refer to the distribution of resources, as does the principle of fairness, but to the access to basic vital opportunities. In this sense, it allows us to include in the public conception of justice the subjective claims of individuals, such as the right to life, well-being, sociability and culture (not the consumption of cultural products, of course, but cultural activity in its most fundamental sense, including for instance participation in politics, language, religion, or the symbolic life of the community). In liberal theories, many of these rights are usually disregarded with the argument that they are common goods that breach the neutrality of a public conception of justice. We have already seen, however, that their inclusion, being fundamental aspects of cohabitation, is well justified. From an ecopolitical point of view, sustainability of cohabitation is a common good for all inhabitants precisely because it allows them to realise these vital opportunities. It is quite reasonable therefore that the principles of justice, in so far as they have to regulate the sustainability of cohabitation by agreement of the parties in the original position, should ensure a certain equality in the access to vital opportunities. In fact, the notion of vital opportunities stems directly from the primary goods that guide the deliberations of these same parties: life (survival), autonomy (well-being), reciprocity (sociability), and friendship (culture). In the artefact of the social contract we are always turning within a kind of circle. It would be awkward if the contract would not reflect in one way or another our own assumptions. As long as these assumptions are well justified, we can be confident that the result will also be justified and that the circle will not be vicious, but rather virtuous.

Being derived from the ties of friendship, the principle of care allows us therefore to take into consideration the subjective hurts that remain outside the principle of fairness (derived from the ties of reciprocity). This means in practice that subjective hurts, even if they do not give rise to valid claims of distributive justice, may give rise to valid claims of vital justice. As some feminist theories rightly point out, justice should thus take into account the needs of all those who lack sufficient autonomy or capacity to fully participate in social cooperation, such as infant, disabled or non-human inhabitants. The principle of care recognises that all inhabitants have the right to claim from the community an equal access to vital opportunities, regardless of their autonomy or capacity to engage in reciprocal relations, as long as maintaining this inequality is not to the greatest benefit of the community as a whole. This condition is important, because we are speaking here of a public principle of justice, not of an ethical or moral duty that would bear on the private behaviour of individuals. If we accept, for instance, that all children have in justice the same rights of care, in so far as the community as a whole would not benefit from caring unequally of children, child care ceases to be a mere parental duty and becomes also a duty of the entire community, giving rise to concrete rights and obligations in the legal arrangement of society. The same could be said of the elderly, disabled, non-human animals, other biological organisms, and so on. It should be pointed out that the principle of care does not contradict in any way all the other principles: elderly people, for instance, could have the right to be taken care by the community without this right infringing on any of the other rights they may have acquired by virtue of the principles of liberty and fairness. Thanks to this third principle of justice, the duty of care does not fall exclusively upon benevolent individuals (usually women), who sustain sick relatives or their children, but becomes a regulatory principle for the entire habitat-nation. How exactly this principle will be applied in practice, for example to protect vulnerable sectors of human society, cultural habits relevant for the community, non-human species threatened with extinction or degraded natural habitats, will depend on the particular circumstances of habitation and on the legislative arrangements of each political community.

The principles of liberty, fairness and care are, in summary, the constitutional foundations of the habitat-nation. These principles have been derived strictly from the contractual mechanism of the liberal theory, without introducing any perfectionist notion of the common good which could not be reasonably justified in a hypothetical original position. Yet, the ecopolitical constitution that emerges from these principles differs in some essential points, such as the adoption of ecological justice and the ethic of care, from the constitutions usually derived from the principles of social or egalitarian liberalism. At the same time, however, there are significant points of coincidence between these constitutions, such as the guarantee of individual liberties or the regulation of distributive justice. Of course, we would still need to elaborate in more detail the principles of liberty and fairness, as well as the articulation of the three principles on the basis of priority rules like the ones suggested by Rawls. In this sense, the priority of liberty in respect to fairness, and of fairness in respect to care, would be perfectly acceptable from the perspective of the ecopolitical theory. It would only be necessary to further clarify how these rules should be applied in the transition from the original position to the constitutional stage and from there to the legislative stage. Since we still need to develop their implications for the organisation of the political community, it might be sufficient for the time being with this general exposition of the principles that should ideally guide the constitution of the habitat-nation.

8 A Community of Free Inhabitants

A habitat-nation will not begin its constitution with "we the people", but rather with "we the inhabitants of...". It is not in the *demos*, a people or a nation postulated as a substantial entity, where the legitimacy of the ecopolitical community lies, but in the inhabitants themselves, the individuals of all species that cohabit in a certain habitat. According to their implicit social contract, these inhabitants have arranged themselves in constitutional orders (vital, individual, social, political) and are bound to each other by the principles of justice (liberty, fairness, care), with the ultimate end of sustaining their common habitation.

More than a democracy (the government of the people), the institutional expression of the inhabitants' political will should be properly called a philiocracy (the government of friends), in so far as all inhabitants, regardless of the differences and conflicts that pull them apart, form a single political community founded on their deliberate choice of living together. Even if the inhabitants have not explicitly chosen to live together, the political institutions that regulate their cohabitation will only be legitimate if the inhabitants have deliberately chosen them. A philiocracy must therefore provide the necessary mechanisms to ensure that the constitutional precepts and the political institutions derived from them are not just acceptable but effectively accepted by a broad majority of inhabitants. Lacking this tacit agreement to live together, manifested in the explicit approval of the constitution and in the day-to-day renewal of the constitutional pact, the habitat-nation can only be a legal fiction.

Clearly, not all inhabitants will have the same capacity to participate in the political constitution of the habitat-nation. In effect, only the inhabitants of the political order will be able to deliberately choose the foundations and the institutions that should regulate the common habitation. Applying the principle of reasonable discrimination, the habitat-nation is thus constituted by the will of the inhabitants of the political order. However, this does not exclude from the political community all the other inhabitants, whether human or non-human, who are unable to make a deliberate choice. It is therefore essential for the philiocratic regime to establish effective institutional mechanisms, such as a system of representation by proxy or some form of statutory or procedural protection, in order to ensure that the legitimate interests of these inhabitants are adequately taken into account in the formation and application of the laws. Whatever the solution adopted in practice, the habitat-nation cannot exclude its most vulnerable inhabitants from the processes of decision-making without immediately losing its legitimacy and reason for being. For clarity's sake, and to the extent that the principles and mechanisms of a philiocracy, necessarily restricted to the inhabitants with political capacity, will tend to approach the principles and mechanisms that generally regulate the democratic systems, I may often refer to philiocracy with the usual and widely-recognised term of democracy.

The practical articulation of this democratic or philiocratic system of government will largely depend on the circumstances of each habitat-nation and we should avoid, as mentioned earlier, the temptation to give general recipes for all political communities. It is nonetheless possible to prescribe the key principles that should ideally guide the formation and articulation of an ecopolitical constitution, even if we avoid entering into the details of such an articulation. Briefly, the principles that will sustain in practice a community of free inhabitants are participation, concordance and reflection. To the extent that these practical principles have been largely derived from the ecoliberal principles of justice agreed by the parties in the original position, it would be reasonable, if we accept the latter, to accept the former as well. As we move from the realm of theoretical to practical principles, however, we are bound to find many more situations where the ecopolitical notions run into difficulties and require us to make choices or accept certain trade-offs. In this sense, and before exposing the principles in some detail, it is useful to bear in mind what we could call the golden rule of ecopolitical practice. This rule states simply that "a policy is good insofar as it sustains cohabitation".

The question of the participation of citizens (or inhabitants, in ecopolitical terms) in the government of the political community has been at the centre of the debate as long as there has been an explicit interest in the possibilities and the limits of collective action. We have already seen that Aristotle defined the *polites* as the person (or rather, the man with properties) who had "the capacity to rule and be ruled" (*to dinasthai arkhein kai arkhesthai*). In this classical context, democracy could be distinguished from other forms of political organisation, like oligarchy or monarchy, by the fact that democratic institutions allowed all *polites* (the *demos*) to effectively exercise their capacity to rule (*kratos*). Participation could be thus defined as the exercise or the realisation of a capacity (*dynamis*) which constitutes the essential attribute of the *polites*. A community of free individuals is, in this sense, the political community that allows the effective participation of its members in the formation and application of collective decisions.

Throughout the history of democracy and its substitutes, this ideal of effective participation has often been the object of severe restrictions, to the point that Aristotle would have been thunderstruck at seeing what kind of political organisations were named democracies, particularly in modern times. This process of transformation of democracy into a strictly regulated method of containing the will of the *demos* reached its high point after the Second World War with the consolidation of the theory of competitive elitism. According to Joseph Schumpeter, democracy is little more than the "institutional arrangement for arriving at political decisions in which individuals acquire the power to decide by means of a competitive struggle for the people's vote". Participation in this system, which continues to be ours, is largely limited to choosing every now and then amongst a handful of candidates and hoping that they will use their power for the common good. Rather than representative democracy, therefore, it would be more accurate to describe such a system as an elective oligarchy.

I cannot discuss here in any depth the theoretical and empirical justifications that sustain the institutional configuration of modern democratic regimes. It is important to remark, however, that there are hardly any coherent arguments today to justify a system of political organisation that restricts so drastically the participation of citizens in the formation of collective decisions. Many theorists have repeatedly pointed out the need to develop the political institutions that would allow citizens to effectively exercise their democratic potential. If these reforms have not yet been put into practice is partly due to the many interests created around the current system of representation, such as the political parties themselves, which constitute a real bastion against change. The problem is nonetheless much deeper. Even before the development of the party system, the Founding Fathers of the United States designed a political regime that restricted to the bare minimum the political participation of citizens, in so far as it was necessary to legitimise the new political order while making sure that the majority vote would not threaten the structure of property and the capacity of individuals to pursue their economic ends. Moreover, as James Madison argued, this new democracy (or rather, republic) had to function effectively in the context of a state of imperial dimensions. In spite of strongly participative dynamics at the base, the American political system was thus conceived from the beginning to serve the geopolitical and economic needs of the nation-state, and in particular the doctrine of the large state. In this context, the effective participation of citizens was not just impractical, but clearly counterproductive. Many other arguments have been put forward since then, such as the citizens' lack of capacity or interest in political issues, in order to continue to legitimise elective oligarchy, or representative democracy, as the "best possible system of government".

Most of these arguments have little or no validity in the case of a philiocracy. To claim for example that the modern state is too large to support any form of participatory democracy makes no sense in the context of a habitat-nation, circumscribed by ecologically and socially sustainable boundaries. Even here, of course, it would not be possible to develop any form of "face to face" democracy such as the one that may have existed in 5th century Athens; but no one is arguing that the effective participation of inhabitants in the political community should replicate the governance mechanisms of a condominium. In the current stage of technological development, there are many possibilities for the implementation of operational forms of participatory democracy such as electronic voting systems that would allow citizens to directly vote on the laws without the need to delegate their vote to a political representative. Surely, there are good reasons not to replace the mechanism of representation entirely with such a system of direct participation; but it is possible to devise intermediary arrangements in order to articulate both systems of government, representation and participation, more effectively than in the current model of political parties. It is a fallacy, therefore, to argue that this model should be maintained because the alternatives are not feasible. In the context of a habitat-nation, and thanks to the new technologies, all possibilities are in fact open. What is possible, however, is not necessarily right or desirable. We should thus ask ourselves if the active participation of the inhabitants in the formation of public decisions is a legitimate principle of organisation for the ecopolitical community.

In civic or liberal theories of justice, political participation is usually defended on the basis of the principle of liberty. The "principle of (equal) participation", as Rawls argues, "requires that all citizens are to have an equal right to take part in, and to determine the outcome of, the constitutional process that establishes the laws with which they are to comply". In so far as the laws of a territory should regulate the exercise of effective freedom for all individuals, it would be unjust to prevent individuals from taking part in the elaboration of these laws or to prevent them to do so in conditions of equality. This logic determines the substantive articulation of political participation, which is basically circumscribed to the sphere of negative freedoms such as the freedom of expression and the freedom of association, but leaves in indeterminacy other more positive freedoms such as the freedom to access public office or the freedom to influence the formation of laws. This does not mean that liberal theoreticians like Rawls do not also defend these positive liberties, but they often do so from perfectionist or pragmatic arguments, not as an obligation derived from the public principles of justice. From this point of view participation would be an essential element of democracy, but only in so far as it allows citizens to be educated in the civic virtues, to feel bound to a political community, and to accept public decisions as legitimate. For these reasons, as John Stuart Mill argued, "the participation should everywhere be as great as the general degree of improvement of the community will allow". In practice, perfectionist arguments of this sort are never able to justify a broad participation of citizens in civic-liberal regimes. As long as civic virtue, social cohesion and political legitimacy are more or less guaranteed, there is no real reason to extend the sphere of participation beyond the most basic mechanisms such as the sporadic suffrage and the theoretical possibility of having access to public office.

Based on the ecoliberal principles of justice, we may be able to justify the need for a more active participation of the members of the community in the formation and application of the laws that regulate this community, giving thereby an effective value to Mill's recommendations. The principle of care in particular states that "inequalities in the access to vital opportunities between inhabitants are to be arranged so that they are to the greatest benefit of the community as a whole". In the case of the inhabitants of the political order such as humans, one of these vital opportunities is precisely the participation in the political life of the community, in so far as it is an essential element of culture. We should thus ask ourselves whether inequality in the access to politics benefits in any way the community as a whole. If this were the case, as Plato and many other theoreticians have argued, it would be just for some individuals to enjoy more rights of participation than others. If the community does not benefit from this inequality, however, we will have to conclude, according to the principles of justice, that participation should be more equal. Not only that, but equality in participation should be enlarged as much as possible up to the point where the community benefits from maintaining a certain degree of inequality. This assessment, rather than depending on superfluous perfectionist arguments, is grounded on the constitutional principles of the political community. Political participation is no longer a question of mere convenience, but one of justice.

In order to further clarify this idea, we could begin by briefly assessing the most extreme case. In a classical democracy, where all individuals rule and are ruled, for instance through the mechanism of election by chance of public officials, the inhabitants would be in a situation of equality in respect to the vital opportunity of politics. However, if we were to reduce the level of participation, by choosing for example the military commanders according to their capacity and not simply by chance, it is obvious that this change would be to the greatest benefit of the community as a whole. Following the same logic, we would reach a point, not yet determined, where the inequality of participation would be optimal from the point of view of justice.

According to the golden rule of ecopolitical practice, therefore, the participation of inhabitants in the political decisions should be everywhere as great as the sustainability of cohabitation will allow. If we can extend this participation beyond the current limits of representative democracy without undermining cohabitation, there is no justification not to do so. Furthermore, we should extend this participation up to the point where an additional increment may undermine the sustainability of cohabitation. This optimal point cannot be fixed beforehand, but it is obvious that the systems of representative democracy in most contemporary civic-nations today are very far away from such a point. To the extent that inhabitants have the capacity and the will to actively participate in the government of the habitat-nation, there is no justification whatsoever for a system that limits the access to politics to a few selected elites through the closed and generally undemocratic mechanisms of party rule. Politicians tend to defend this system of representation arguing that citizens are not actually too interested in politics. Some political scientists, juggling with the surveys, are even capable of giving so-called empirical arguments to underpin this fallacy of the elitist theory, ignoring the fact that a capacity (*dynamis*) can only be realised under adequate institutional conditions. Where these conditions are absent, any judgement on the will or the disposition of individuals is a pure rumination, founded almost exclusively on the commentator's creativity. And in any case, once inhabitants acquire the effective capacity and not just a theoretical possibility of having an equal access to politics, they should keep the freedom to decide whether to exercise it or not. This is a decision that should always fall on the individual inhabitant and can never be prejudged by the political agents, much less by their corporations. Only in an institutional context that ensures the equal access of all inhabitants to the vital opportunity of politics, whether they choose to realise it or not, can we properly speak of political freedom and therefore of philiocracy.

Of course, this equality in political participation should not be absolute. As mentioned above, there are some inequalities that could benefit the community as a whole and could therefore limit the degree of participation of the inhabitants. Moreover, according to the priority of liberty, it will be necessary to establish additional limits in order to preserve the rights of individuals and of minorities from potential abuses by the majority, as well as to preserve the constitutional foundations of cohabitation and the principles of justice themselves. In particular, the constitution of the habitat-nation should foresee (1) mechanisms of representation and balance of powers (principle of concordance), and (2) mechanisms of deliberation and balance of opinions (principle of reflection). Rather than restrictions, however, these mechanisms should be regarded as ways to enrich participation and improve its quality, with the ultimate end of ensuring the sustainability of the political community. The optimal level of participation in the habitat-nation will thus guarantee the maximum possible equality in the access to the vital opportunity of politics while preserving the sustainability of cohabitation.

Besides the question of participation, perhaps the most fundamental problem of democracy is the inherent tendency of all human groups to organise themselves into factions. An oligarchy or a monarchy does not have to face the problem of factions because they take the faction as a principle of government. In so far as the legitimate political organisation of the community lies more or less substantively on the whole of its members, the problem of factions is indeed a formidable one. It is so intractable that many, like the proponents of the elitist theory, have practically abandoned any attempts to solve it and have opted instead for a definition of democracy so minimalist that it can hardly be accepted as such. According to this formulation, still prevalent today, democracy would no longer be "the government of the people", but "the government of the politicians in the name of (and supposedly also for the benefit of) the people". As with oligarchy and monarchy, however, this is only an apparent solution, given that politicians naturally tend to constitute themselves into a faction so that representative democracy turns easily into elective oligarchy. Elitist theories of democracy do not have to face the problem of factions because the principle of government itself is in fact the faction. That this faction should be elected is no doubt an improvement from absolute monarchy or feudalism; and to the extent that there is effective competition between the factions that struggle for power, the outcome may be more or less satisfactory from the point of view of the voters' generic preferences, as elitist theoreticians never cease to remind us. The fact that a system is satisfactory, however, does not mean that it is just or that this satisfaction could not be significantly improved with a different system. An absolute monarchy may also, if the monarch is attentive enough to the needs of the subjects, constitute a satisfactory government from the point of view of the subjects' generic preferences, as absolutist theoreticians never ceased to remind everyone at the time. Liberals were quite right nonetheless to reply that political systems are not legitimate by virtue of their capacity to satisfy the general needs of individuals but in so far as those individuals regard them as legitimate. They added furthermore, and also with good reason, that the fact that an absolute monarchy is better than a tyranny does not mean that the situation of individuals under an absolute monarchy could not be improved with a different type of government. *Mutatis mutandis*, these replies could also be addressed to elitist theoreticians who still defend elective oligarchy (or representative democracy) because it satisfies acceptably well the generic preferences of citizens and there appears to be no feasible alternative. To this, the ecopolitical theory replies that the preferences of citizens could be satisfied much better with alternative systems of government and that these alternatives are perfectly feasible. If the history of absolutism serves any purpose, perhaps the guardians of the status quo should not disregard us with so much arrogance.

In order for the alternative to be feasible, however, it needs to face the problem of the factions; and to face it, if it wants to be faithful to the ecopolitical principles, without creating another oligarchic faction that would replace the present ones. There are no magical solutions to this problem, but a good start are the checks and balances developed in the initial stages of liberal democracy, particularly in the United States. Nowadays, these mechanisms have generally become fossilised and their efficacy tends to be quite modest, even when judged by the initial aims of their proponents. Yet, the idea of designing constitutional checks and balances in order to restrain and concord the different powers of the state continues to be a perfectly valid one. Concordance is thus one of the practical principles that should guide the constitutional design of the habitat-nation. It must be stressed, however, that concordance is not the same as concord. Concordance is a constant but never accomplished tension that strives for the equilibrium of the whole political system, in spite of the different forces that pull it apart and tend to discord it. It implies therefore a certain disposition to the accord or agreement between the parties, but also the existence of solid institutional mechanisms to prevent the formation of structural imbalances that may undermine the sustainability of cohabitation. Here I will mostly refer to those mechanisms, but we should not forget that institutions are like corals; without a dynamic and plural society inhabiting them, they become little more than calcareous skeletons abandoned like monuments at the bottom of the sea.

In one of the foundational documents of modern democracy, *Federalist* article number 10, Madison pointed out that the young American republic should be articulated in a way that would prevent the formation of both minority and majority factions. In so far as Madison was also trying to preserve the rights of the minority of owners against the threat posed by a large majority of non-owners, while creating a large state that could become in time a commercial empire, the solutions he puts forward are clearly deficient from a democratic point of view. "If a faction consists of less than a majority", he claims, "relief is supplied by the republican principle, which enables the majority to defeat its sinister views by regular vote". Madison does not say much more on the subject, but it is quite obvious that this "republican principle" is totally insufficient to protect majorities from influential minorities, whether they are interest groups or the same oligarchic structures of political parties.

Not surprisingly, Madison is much more explicit when it comes to establishing the mechanisms that should protect minorities from the majority. The system of representation on the one hand, and a political community of large dimensions on the other should serve, or so he claims, to prevent or contain the formation of a majority faction that could threaten the different minorities. Needless to say, republican or elitist theoreticians tend to exaggerate this threat, while understating or ignoring altogether the threat implied by the formation of influential minority factions, which is nonetheless much more common. A well-organised philiocracy, however, must take this risk of populist or demagogic drift very seriously, as an eventual tyranny of the majority could easily breach individual rights and liberties, ignore the legitimate demands of minorities, or modify in its own interest the political institutions that sustain cohabitation. In this sense, Madison's argument in favour of a representative system of government is certainly sound, but we would also need to establish clear limits to this representation in order to avoid the formation of minority factions that could control the state at the majority's expense. Liberal theoreticians tend to forget that it is as important to protect minorities from the majority as to protect the majority from minorities. In regards to the second mechanism of control, Madison's argument is so biased by his imperial ambitions, a key underlying motif in the whole debate with the anti-federalists, that it is hardly able to stand any ground. An increase in the size of the political community does not ensure in any way that such a community will be open and plural. On the contrary, it will often tend to make it much less so. There is no denying that the risk of formation or expansion of oppressive majorities is strongly diminished in a plural society. This pluralism does not depend, however, on the size of the community, but rather on its internal dynamism. An active philial society, with a plurality of associations effectively channelling the different opinions, sensibilities and interests of the inhabitants, is an essential element of concordance, as it substantially limits the risk or the negative effects of majority factions. This is precisely the strength of the political regimes of some small states such as Denmark, Sweden or the Netherlands, which have developed consensual models of democracy where pluralism and dissent become an integral part of the political process. Large states, on the contrary, tend to prefer systems where a strong parliamentary majority is able to neutralise internal divergence on fundamental questions such as the existence of the state itself, while fostering the homogenisation of society under a more or less coercive nation-building project. In this context, far from being valued, internal diversity is actually perceived by the elites, even when they have been democratically elected, as an obstacle for the unity and power of the state. Its reduction or neutralisation becomes thus a question of national interest. In large states, therefore, democracy may fall with greater ease than in smaller states to demagogy and populism, giving way in some extreme cases to the dreadful tyranny of the majority. This is shown quite clearly by the cases of pre-war Germany and Italy, which could hardly be described as small parochial communities.

In a philiocracy, the risk that government would fall into the hands of a minority faction (oligarchy) or a majority faction (demarchy) is in principle limited by the reduced scale of the habitat-nation and by the internal dynamism of philial society. These risks are not, however, to be neglected. It is important to understand that these two tendencies draw their strength from an inherent tension of the political system. Thanks to the philial dimension of the habitat-nation, it is possible to significantly extend the regime of participation by the inhabitants in the formation of public decisions. This participation contributes to concordance in so far as it helps to keep in check any oligarchic tendencies. At the same time, however, an increase in participation necessarily strengthens the demarchic tendencies of the political community, as it multiplies the value of the majority principle. Beyond the balancing effect of social pluralism, therefore, the principle of concordance requires the existence of some constitutional checks and balances in order to restrict the power of the majority. These mechanisms should not be derived from a lack of trust in the democratic system, but from the need to uphold its essential processes against the abuses and derivations that may threaten them, whether it is a minority exploiting them in its own benefit or a majority misusing the power it has gained thanks to its numerical superiority.

A philiocracy like Ulysses' ship must always navigate between oligarchy and demarchy, without forgetting however that one and the other are never found with the same frequency nor have the same consequences. Too often, the liberal mistrust of the majority principle seems to respond to particular interests rather than to the real threat of demagogic or populist drift. Of course, the decision of the majority is not always the best decision. Majorities as much as minorities do make mistakes; they even make many mistakes. In some extreme cases majorities may even become as tyrannical as some minorities. Instead of turning democracy into a fetish, we must therefore give an adequate justification to the right value of the democratic principle and establish the necessary institutional mechanisms to prevent the majority from imposing its law over the common good of the sustainability of cohabitation. This does not mean renouncing the majority principle, nor the largest possible framework of political participation of the inhabitants compatible with sustainability. The decision based on a majority vote is not justified by its heuristic virtues, but because it is the most legitimate way of organising collective decision-making and therefore the most sustainable in the context of a political community founded on the principles of justice. A decision taken by a majority of inhabitants is not legitimate because it automatically represents the will of all inhabitants, but because it is the result of the free, equal and deliberate participation of all inhabitants in the democratic process. While the majority may certainly be wrong, its mistakes are the mistakes of the whole political community, in so far as they stem from procedures of decision generally accepted by all inhabitants. In the context of a philiocracy, we should thus vindicate the right to be wrong, without which there would not be the possibility of being right.

Against the majority principle, and often against democracy in general, elitist or aristocratic theories tend to defend at least since Plato the idea that the majority is not capable of taking collective decisions by itself and it is therefore necessary for the common good that a qualified minority should "be at the helm". When discussing this question, however, there is the tendency to mingle into the same argument three questions that should be kept apart: the capacity of public servants, the capacity of political representatives, and the capacity of political organisations.

In modern societies, characterised by a considerable degree of complexity, it is quite evident that public servants should be qualified to perform their task. A professional bureaucracy is a necessity in all modern political systems, whether they are oligarchic, democratic or philiocratic. It would be absurd, therefore, to pretend that inhabitants should rule the habitat-nation at this level of implication. On another level, however, the Platonic or elitist argument claims that political representatives, not just public servants, should also be qualified to perform their task, even to the point of being professionals of politics. In general, the theory of the habitat-nation is not opposed to this line of reasoning. As mentioned above, in so far as it is to the greatest benefit of the community as a whole that political offices should be occupied by the best qualified and not just by any inhabitant picked at random, the principle of care allows us to justify the need for an unequal access to the vital opportunity of politics. Nonetheless, it should be remarked that the community does not benefit from the mere fact that politicians are professionals, but only to the extent that this professionalism is able to guarantee, at least in principle, that political offices will be occupied by the best qualified amongst all inhabitants. If professionalism implies for whatever reason that the best qualified are kept out of political office, while professional politicians allot these offices to themselves according to meritocratic criteria restricted to their own group or according to some other form of allocation (nepotism, favouritism, and so on), there is no justification whatsoever to maintain such a system. A group of professional politicians who occupy most public offices according to corporatist criteria by unjustifiably restraining the inhabitants' access to politics should be properly described as a political caste or faction.

The problem in this case is not so much the capacity of individual politicians as the institutional regime of selection, circulation and distribution of the political function, which in current political systems has been arrogated by organisations of an inherently oligopolistic nature, the political parties. Of course, from a formal point of view any citizen may become a politician nowadays. In reality, however, a citizen who wishes to effectively function as a politician needs to become first a member of a political party and submit to the internal mechanisms of access, promotion and discipline that regulate these corporations. Considering that there are important barriers of entry for new parties and that competition between existing parties is strictly governed by the laws promulgated by these same parties, it is quite clear that these organisations tend to form a classical oligopolistic structure or cartel. In order to fully realise the vital opportunity of politics, therefore, individuals have no other choice but to militate in one of the majority political parties, in so far as the alternatives such as the militancy in minority parties or the creation of new parties are rarely feasible in practice; and even if they were, the reality is that any political party that manages to attain some degree of representation in the current institutional system tends to develop very quickly the same hierarchical structures that characterise the other parties. In a sense, this is a consequence of the "iron law of oligarchy" formulated a long time ago by Robert Michels and still to be refuted. "By a universally applicable social law", he wrote, "every organ of the collectivity, brought into existence through the need for the division of labour, creates for itself, as soon as it becomes consolidated, interests peculiar to itself. The existence of these special interests involves a necessary conflict with the interests of the collectivity". Without an effective constitutional regulation, therefore, parties easily become tyrannies in the hands of minorities who tend to use their political power to their own benefit or to the benefit of the corporation. To speak of the capacity of politicians in this oligopolistic context could perhaps be a funny joke if it were not for the fact that these same cartels are actually ruling the destinies of most nations. The restriction of the political function to the best qualified of inhabitants is thus partially justified on the basis of the ecoliberal principles of justice, but there is no need to invoke those principles to realise that the best are rarely found in the oligopolistic structures of the political parties. Under these conditions, the words of Rousseau have not lost any of its pertinence, if only we substitute "monarchies" with "political parties": "Those who succeed in [the political parties] are most frequently only petty mischief-makers, petty crooks, petty intriguers, whose petty talents, which enable them to climb to high posts in [the political parties], only serve to show the public their ineptitude as soon as they have attained them".

Even if the habitat-nation were to maintain some form of representation, the inhabitants' access to the vital opportunity of politics should never depend so entirely on oligopolistic organisations capable of misusing the institutional regime to achieve their own particular purposes to the expense of the common good of cohabitation. Philiocracy does not mean the government of the friends of a given political party's chairman or secretary general, but the government of all friends; that is, all inhabitants in so far as they are bound by the deliberate choice of living together. A political community incapable of generating individuals with enough capacity to rule and legislate without having to resort to a specialised caste of politicians is doomed for serfdom. While not everyone should access the political function, it is essential that this access be regulated by an open and transparent regime of selection and circulation, in order to ensure a real competition for the different public offices, founded on merit and capability, not on social or economic resources. Moreover, these offices should be subject to a certain rotation to avoid the formation of endogamous and power-addicted elites. In any case, an open access to the vital opportunity of politics does not mean giving up the good politicians; it is just a matter of recognising that good politicians originate in society as a whole, not in the restricted apparatuses of a handful of parties. The health of philiocracy largely depends on its ability to promote a permanent fertilisation between society and politics, instead of separating them into two antagonistic spheres. The talent in philial society should filter through to the political institutions and political talent should revert back to philial society. Good captains are an asset of the habitat-nation, but they should not be allowed to take possession of the ship.

In a dynamic and plural philial society, the capacity of inhabitants to understand and deliberate over the political problems of their habitat-nation should be above all doubt. In such a context, the diversity of political opinions and projects could be adequately channelled through political associations as long as they are effectively prevented through institutional mechanisms from falling into the "iron law of oligarchy". This regulation should ensure in particular that

(1) there is real competition between political associations (to avoid oligopolistic competition),

(2) the associations have open and democratic internal structures (to avoid oligopolistic governance), and

(3) the political associations and the electoral processes rely exclusively on transparent and strictly supervised financial sources (to avoid oligopolistic influence).

All these norms should be included in the constitution of the habitat-nation in order to prevent political associations from modifying them in their own interest. While recognising their merits, we should never forget the inherent tendency of any representative organisation to become an oligarchic faction. It is essential therefore to treat political associations as potential threats to the sustainability of philiocracy. Of course, the efficacy of all these institutional mechanisms is rather limited where organisations may attain such a large influence on society thanks to the mass media. It is thus necessary to establish additional checks and balances, for example by allowing inhabitants to arbitrate with their vote on those legislative and executive initiatives that fail to obtain a sufficient consensus amongst political representatives. In this way, the inhabitants would effectively become the fourth power of the state, together with the legislative, executive and judiciary, completing thereby the constitutional architecture of the habitat-nation.

Terms like philiocracy or philial society may easily induce the error of thinking that we are somehow minimising or understating the conflicts derived from social diversity and from the plurality of opinions, sensibilities, values, habits or vital conditions of the inhabitants. Where a habitat-nation is ecologically and socially coherent, its inhabitants share certain habits and certain forms of habitation which allow them to cohabit in a sustainable manner.

In this context, the formation of a philial society is a relatively smooth process, in so far as inhabitants assume the deliberate choice of living together as an almost natural fact. This does not mean, far from it, that philial society is free from conflict and tension. Inhabitants may have deliberately chosen to live together and this is the meaning of friendship according to Aristotle, but they continue to maintain deep discrepancies over the manner of organising this cohabitation, over the effective application of the common principles of justice, over the persons who should hold public office, and over many other collective decisions which can only be settled through the political process. In a habitat-nation, therefore, all inhabitants agree that it is necessary to preserve the sustainability of cohabitation. This common good is the foundation of the political community and allows it to develop into a philiocracy. They may not agree, however, on the means that should be employed to achieve it, not even on the specific objectives that this sustainability entails. Agreement is never a pre-existing property of philial society, but the potential outcome of interdependencies and daily relationships between inhabitants. Public institutions can make a decisive contribution to concordance by promoting the widest possible consensus between the different sectors of the philial society; but concordance should never be taken for granted, much less if it serves to hide the real conflicts of society such as class, religion or gender, as well as the discriminations derived from them.

We need to recognise, therefore, that the interrelations between inhabitants may produce agreement but also disagreement. Philial society, to the extent that it is open and plural, is permanently hanging in a fragile and unstable balance, which requires public institutions attentive to the conflicts and injustices, as well as political actors capable of responding to the demands of the different groups of inhabitants.

In a well-organised philiocracy, however, institutional concordance cannot guarantee by itself that the pluralism of philial society will be adequately channelled through the political system, nor does it allow inhabitants to ensure that the internal processes of this system effectively sustain cohabitation. In order to redress the shortcomings of institutions and balance the constitutional structure of the habitat-nation, we need a third practical principle. This principle of reflection has two separate dimensions: (1) reflection as deliberation, and (2) reflection as transparency.

The majority principle, as pointed out by democracy's critics but also by the proponents of new deliberative forms of democracy, tends to focus too much on vote-aggregation without effectively incorporating the complexity of the process that leads to the vote. Current electoral systems assume that voters are equivalent to consumers and that voting is the rational selection of alternatives on the basis of individual preferences. This rational-instrumental model ignores the complex process through which individuals form their political opinion by dialogically interacting with other individuals and with the discourses of the public sphere. Voters do not limit themselves to voting, but adjust their vote through a process of deliberation or reflection in a plural social context. Lately, some theoreticians have insisted on the need to transform the electoral systems in order to incorporate, beyond the mechanisms of vote aggregation (vote-centric), more innovative mechanisms of collective discussion and debate (talk-centric). They hope in this way to correct the tendency of civic democracies to transform the political arena into a supermarket where the voters-consumers are expected to fill up their trolleys with the pre-packaged discourses of the political parties and the mass media. As long as they do not modify the structural conditions of democracy, however, these reforms are bound to play a very trivial role, like those stands that multinationals set up in front of supermarkets to ask for the opinion of consumers and to make them feel for a brief moment as if their reflections were really taken into account.

In a philiocracy, the extension of participation would necessarily require the adoption of effective mechanisms of public deliberation in order to integrate the plurality of philial society into the political process. This would ensure that the majority principle is applied in a reasonable manner and reflects the views shared by all inhabitants. The existence of public channels where political discrepancies may be settled without confrontation, by exchanging arguments and points of view, is an important condition for the stability of the habitat-nation. Indeed, friends argue; they may even have incompatible opinions on fundamental aspects of their cohabitation; but these discrepancies should not be so deep as to break up the ties that justify their friendship. In so far as they constitute an effective political community, bound by the deliberate choice of living together, inhabitants should have the capacity and the opportunity to openly and reasonably disagree on any question that may affect their cohabitation or the state of the habitat-nation. All public decisions should thus be founded on a previous and broad debate where everyone has had the opportunity to be heard on a free and equal standing. This is the only way of preserving an open and plural philial society, a political community where inhabitants make every day the deliberate choice of living together in spite of the differences and discrepancies that will inevitably keep them apart.

The implementation of these instruments of public deliberation in civic democracies often stumbles upon the lack of fundamental consensus that could effectively bind together the members of the political community. When individuals do not want to live together, there is no framework of dialogue that will concord their opinions, as every couple in the process of getting a divorce knows too well. Only a political community founded on the sustainability of cohabitation, such as the habitat-nation, may be able to develop deliberative forms of democracy which strengthen the plurality of society without weakening its cohesion. Lacking this plurality, there can be no real deliberation; but lacking a common framework, deliberation quickly degenerates into confrontation and division. It should be clear, however, that deliberation can never replace the vote. Deliberation informs and improves voters' opinions, but political decisions should still be adopted, according to the public norms that regulate the philiocratic system, on the basis of the binding vote of a majority of inhabitants. Once a free, open and equal deliberation has taken place and everyone has had the chance of being reasonably heard, the decision of the majority is more easily accepted by everyone, even by those who have lost the vote. On the contrary, an indefinite deliberation or the pretension to achieve some kind of consensus will only lead to frustration, conflict and the dissolution of philial society.

There can be no effective deliberation, however, as long as the informational asymmetries between institutions and inhabitants have not been reduced to the minimum. Transparency is thus an essential requisite of the philiocratic system of government. Under the constitution of the habitat-nation, political institutions should be accountable and convey to the inhabitants sufficient and faithful information on all public questions, so that they may be able to effectively participate in the political decisions of the community. Moreover, transparency is not just a matter of public institutions, but should be extended to the whole of the public sphere and to the philial society itself. A free and plural press, for instance, is a crucial element of reflection in so far as it allows inhabitants to watch over the actions of their government and representatives. It will also help inhabitants to develop an informed and reasoned opinion on the problems of the habitat-nation, so that they may contribute to a well-argued public deliberation. The constitution of the habitat-nation must therefore establish the necessary legal mechanisms to preserve the plurality of public information in all its dimensions, actively preventing the formation of media oligopolies which may threaten the equal access of all inhabitants to the vital opportunity of politics.

Another important role of public transparency is the prevention, control and fight against the corruption of the political system. Corruption, it should be very clear, is the cancer of the political community. With corruption, as with tumours, tolerance is not an option. One cannot just let a tumour be; it must be extirpated. To think that a small amount of corruption is acceptable as long as the political system functions reasonably well is an audacity with often fatal results. A tumour, no matter how benign it may seem, if it is not extirpated in time, may spread to the whole organism, driving it to decomposition and death. What is at stake in corruption is not ethics or efficiency, but the survival of the habitat-nation, and eventually of any form of political community founded on the principles of justice. The constitution of the habitat-nation must therefore establish the necessary institutional mechanisms to watch as strictly as possible over all the powers of the state and take legal action in each and every case of corruption that may surface. As in many other instances, an independent judiciary system is thus an essential element of a healthy political community. Of course, these legal arrangements will always be insufficient. Corruption, like the cancerous mutations that upset the healthiest of organisms, is never at rest. Only the constant vigilance of the inhabitants themselves may prevent and mitigate its effects. As long as philial society is dynamic and plural, the inhabitants are well-informed and have adequate institutional mechanisms to participate in the political decisions of the habitat-nation, the fight against corruption is a war that can be won and must be won.

9

Inhabiting the World

The ecopolitical articulation of the social and biological community that I am describing here under the concept of the habitat-nation is not just a theoretical construction, but aims to serve, to the extent that the inhabitants democratically decide to adopt it, as a guide for the constitution of real political units capable of effectively evolving in the current world and of sustaining themselves in the long term. In this sense, it is important to point out the distinctive contributions of the habitat-nation in relation to the two main models of geopolitical articulation of the political community prevalent at the moment, the nation-state and cosmopolitanism. Between these two models, often swamped by a lack of definition, there is also the supranational or continental construction, which in practice may adopt different forms, from a mere commercial or military coordination of nation-states to more ambitious projects of economic and political integration. Here, I will attempt to place the habitat-nation in the context of these projects, in order to demonstrate that an ecopolitical community could overcome many of their deficiencies and stand up as an alternative model for the future.

In the modern world, we can roughly identify three main geopolitical forms: small nations, large states and even larger empires. This classification is based on the territorial and demographic scale of the countries, but it also implies some distinctions in relation to the political organisation and the degree of ethnic homogeneity of the different communities. Empires would thus be very large political units such as the United States, China or Russia, often with a diverse population and complex forms of political and territorial organisation. Large states such as France, Nigeria or Argentina tend to be smaller and more homogeneous than empires, even if they still have considerable dimensions and often also ethnic minorities more or less integrated under an assimilationist or pluriethnic political project. Finally, small nations are political units of small size such as Denmark, Jordan or Kerala, with a relatively homogeneous population and a considerable degree of political cohesion, even if they do not necessarily constitute sovereign states. Like any typology, this one has some problems of internal coherence and external validity. As a panoramic vision of the geopolitical diversity of the world, however, it allows us to highlight some essential facts. Firstly, two out of three people in today's world live in small-scale political units (small nations), whether under regimes of autonomy in relation to the large states or with a state of their own. These communities tend to have a significant degree of internal cohesion and cooperation, even if they do not identify themselves as nations. Yet, international politics continues to be largely based on the post-Westphalian system of states, according to which only the political communities constituted as sovereign states may have representation in multilateral organisms such as the United Nations, and effectively participate in the elaboration of regional or global policies. At the same time, however, economic globalisation, driven by technological change and the growing integration of international trade, is pushing states of medium to large size to seek alliances and forms of coordination with other states in order to compete with already existing empires. These projects of supranational empire-building, the most significant of which is of course the European Union, can only be sustained by an increasing transfer of sovereignty from the states to the larger units. From a wide perspective, therefore, this process seems to lead to the formation of new geopolitical structures with a degree of economic, political and military integration comparable to imperial states. Adopting a more neutral terminology, we could say that the present world is geopolitically configured on the basis of

(1) small-sized units with strong internal cohesion and weak sovereignty;

(2) mid-sized units with weak internal cohesion and decreasing sovereignty;

(3) large-sized units with very weak internal cohesion and increasing sovereignty.

Basically, sovereignty is the capacity to exercise legal power over a territory and a population (jurisdiction) on the basis of internal recognition (legitimacy) and external recognition (independence). This capacity derives in part from the interstate structure, which sanctions a certain configuration of the system of states, and in part from the degree of internal cohesion of each political community. This explains why the ideology of the nation-state (nationalism) that still serves to justify present-day liberal or republican states has always tried to assimilate or homogenise its population. In spite of the state's coercive action, social cohesion in most nation-states (the mid-sized units) is generally weak and the forms of political articulation of the community inevitably tend to restrict direct participation. On the contrary, the small units have in general much more social cohesion and are thus able to develop more participatory forms of political articulation. "The more the social bond is extended", as Rousseau wrote, "the more it is weakened; and, in general, a small state is proportionally stronger than a large one".

In the context of the process of globalisation, however, the tendency is precisely to extend as far as possible the social bond, with the consolidation or formation of supranational or continental structures. These large-sized political units should in time replace the mid-sized units, which are no longer economically viable and are less able to guarantee social cohesion than the small units. The lack of social cohesion in the large-sized units, however, poses serious problems to their democratic legitimacy, especially in a context where the cost of forcing this cohesion with nationalistic policies, such as the ones traditionally adopted by large states, is just no longer bearable. Contemporary geopolitics is thus caught in a dilemma, trapped between the economic need to consolidate the large-sized units and the inherent incapacity of these units to maintain social cohesion and therefore the democratic legitimacy of the political system. The promotion of citizenship and civic virtues, an increasingly common response in all vertical discourses, can hardly conceal the fact that citizens in these large units lack any effective political potential beyond their marginal participation in an increasingly diluted regime of vote aggregation. As long as the principle of legitimation of these large units continues to be democracy, and this is something that should never be taken for granted, the lack of participation will weigh heavily on their development. The problem is not so much that citizens are unable to effectively participate in the government of these large political communities, but the fact that citizens who do not participate are also citizens who do not trust; and this lack of trust is fatal for the efficiency of the whole system, which depends to a large extent on the active acquiescence of the population in order to minimise the costs of supervision, control and coercion. The democratic solution to this problem would of course require the political articulation of the large and small-sized units (renouncing the mid-sized ones), with a significant devolution of sovereignty to the latter, in order to preserve at the same time the meaningful political communities and the mechanisms of supranational or continental coordination. In this sense, the habitat-nation postulates itself as a model for the political articulation of the small-sized units which could replace the currently dominant nation-state and promote the consolidation of the large-sized units on more democratic and sustainable foundations.

As we have seen, the theory of the habitat-nation explains why the optimal scale of the political community approximately corresponds to the small-sized geopolitical units and not to the mid or large-sized ones. The fundamental criterion that justifies the existence of a particular habitat-nation is the social and ecological sustainability of cohabitation. The coincidence of a human and a biological community in a habitat on which both of them depend for their access to vital opportunities is the best guarantee that individual autonomy, cooperative reciprocity and philial care will promote the regeneration of the habits and forms of habitation shared by the inhabitants of a particular community. The theory of the nation-state, on the contrary, justifies the existence of a political community on the exclusive basis of a human community defined in terms of supposedly pre-existing ethnic bonds. Its indifference towards the ecological sustainability of the common habitat gives way to nation-states that are too small to sustain themselves (Singapore, Liechtenstein, Monaco) or too large for the human community to effectively sustain the biological community (Spain, United Kingdom, India). Furthermore, the social sustainability of these large states tends to be also quite precarious. Many of them include significant national or ethnic minorities, in so far as they have been built through processes of military or political assimilation which have not taken into account the diversity, not only of the natural environment, but also of the human populations. The formation of these large states has been generally motivated by the need to secure a large market and a sufficient military force to maintain it in the context of fierce interstate competition. This logic is insensible to the ties and interdependencies that bind inhabitants together and tends to generate strong imbalances that undermine the social and ecological sustainability of the different communities. Large states, even those that more closely approach the theoretical model of the nation-state, are incapable of sustaining democratic regimes with a minimum degree of participation and must develop systems of representation that tend to alienate inhabitants from public life, inducing a permanent degree of instability, mistrust and lack of legitimacy in the political system. The estrangement of inhabitants from their government, as well as the estrangement of inhabitants from each other that the abstract identification with the state or the nation tends to foster, makes it easier for political systems to fall under the influence of interest groups, who can use their power to promote policies that go against the sustainability of human and biological communities. In short, the nation-state is a highly dysfunctional political model both from a social and an ecological point of view.

According to the ecopolitical theory, we should thus renounce once and for all the model of the nation-state and the practice of building large states. These states, even when they have fairly democratic institutions, are not able to sustain forms of cohabitation based on the principles of justice and do not allow inhabitants to actively participate in the government of their community. It is somewhat surprising, therefore, that the existence of large states continues to be justified on the basis of liberal principles, considering their obvious incapacity to give a satisfactory response to citizens' demands of freedom and equality. It should be remarked, in this sense, that the systematic concealment by liberal theorists of the dysfunctions inherent in current models of nation-building stems from a dilemma that cannot be resolved without profound changes in the conception of the modern state. If liberals want to achieve, as they claim, higher levels of political participation in a democratic system of government that respects individual freedoms, they must give up the nation-state, and especially the large states. Cosmopolitan critics are right to denounce that liberal nationalism betrays its universalistic principles by remaining loyal to a political framework so obviously particularistic and arbitrary as the nation-state. Liberal theorists, however, are quite right to point out that cosmopolitanism is a utopian and impracticable option, precisely because the ties between individuals are always particular even if the principles might be universal. This debate shows, in any case, that liberalism finds itself in an almost insolvable contradiction. The problem could be summarised in schematic terms: (1) cosmopolitanism is the inevitable political consequence of liberal principles, (2) cosmopolitanism is not grounded on natural foundations and is thus impracticable, (3) accepting the alternative of a political community grounded on the common good means to renounce the universal principles of justice and therefore liberalism, (4) liberals, if they want to remain as such and avoid the siren calls of utopia, must assume the defence of the nation-state, even if it is only for pragmatic or strategic reasons. What liberals do not understand is that point 3 is actually false. As I have tried to demonstrate, it is perfectly possible to articulate the political community in a plural society without giving up the guarantees of individual liberty, but incorporating at the same time the common good of the sustainability of cohabitation as a public and universal principle of justice. Rather than continuing to fend for an obsolete and dysfunctional nation-state, liberals should therefore assume that the political community most coherent with their principles, beyond the utopian project of cosmopolitanism, is the habitat-nation.

The habitat-nation, unlike the nation-state, does not claim that political sovereignty lies in the people or the nation, collective entities that have to be defined explicitly or implicitly on the basis of ethnic or arbitrarily delimited territorial boundaries. The concept of sovereignty itself is a doubtful one, since it reflects a non-democratic articulation of the political community and does not correspond any longer with the realities of a world where interdependencies and shared sovereignties are the norm. Thus, the ecopolitical theory prefers to speak of legitimacy, a concept that reflects much better the dynamic and horizontal nature of the relations between inhabitants and their political institutions. In the habitat-nation, political legitimacy is articulated in terms of cohabitation. The ecopolitical community, as I have already discussed in some detail, is constituted by all inhabitants, not as a people or abstract citizens, but as individuals who share habits and forms of habitation. It is the inhabitants, bound together by the ties of autonomy, reciprocity and friendship, who give themselves the political institutions that should sustain the social community and the biological community according to the shared principles of justice.

The philiocratic institutions of the habitat-nation should therefore be more participative and deliberative than current regimes of representative democracy in most civic-nations. The bioregional scale of the community and the degree of cohesion derived from the strong interdependencies between inhabitants, both within the social and the biological communities, facilitate the democratic process and help steer it towards the sustainability of cohabitation. It is a well-known fact that democratic systems, based on the majority principle, function much better when voters trust each other. "If the various sectors of society have reasonable confidence in one another and share a common conception of justice", as Rawls wrote, "the rule by bare majorities may succeed fairly well. To the extent that this underlying agreement is lacking, the majority principle becomes more difficult to justify because it is less probable that just policies will be followed. There may, however, be no procedures that can be relied upon once distrust and enmity pervade society". Certainly, a nation-state may develop a reasonably participatory and legitimate democratic system as long as it is able to maintain both a strong sense of cohesion and sufficient social dynamism. These conditions, however, are only found in a few small nations such as Denmark or the Netherlands, with relatively horizontal systems of representation which are capable at the same time of channelling social plurality and achieving effective agreements. In a small democracy, as Montesquieu wrote, "the interest of the public is more obvious, better understood, and more within the reach of every citizen". As the state increases in size, however, interpersonal trust between the members of the political community inevitably decreases and the government by majority becomes more problematic, especially when there are significant national or ethnic minorities within the state. This is the main reason why large states need to develop complex and vertical mechanisms of political representation which tend to restrict the majority principle. Even those regimes that decentralise some functions in subordinate units, such as federal or regional states, are unable to attend accurately enough to the wills of the different communities that the state subsumes as a matter of principle in the abstract notion of people or nation. As a consequence, citizens are increasingly detached from the government and their political mistrust is ever growing. According to the ecopolitical theory, on the contrary, the political community should be articulated from meaningful social communities bound to a certain natural habitat. The foundation of the habitat-nation is thus the friendship that binds the inhabitants to each other and to a common project of habitation; or as Aristotle said, "the deliberate choice of living together". Sustainability of cohabitation is the common good that strengthens the bonds of the philial society and allows the habitat-nation to develop more efficient, participatory and legitimate democratic institutions than those of the nation-state. After all, humans accept much better the decisions by majority, even if they disagree with them, when they are the result of a vote amongst friends.

Besides enhancing democratic dynamics, the model of the habitat-nation could also help to integrate the cultural diversity of modern societies into the political community without resorting to policies of monocultural assimilation or multicultural compartmentalisation. The nation-state, founded on the postulated unity of the people or the nation, inevitably moves back and forth between these two alternatives as it attempts to uphold the cohesion of the political community. Modern nationalism's efforts of social engineering, whereby the state mobilised all its resources to forge the nation, are no longer applicable in most contemporary societies, characterised by a growing diversity and a keener consciousness of individual and collective rights. The recipes of multiculturalism, on the other hand, are equally questionable, as they tend to reify cultural communities on the basis of rigid categories, often ignoring the pluralism of the actual individuals and groups. The contradictions inherent in these "politics of recognition" are particularly evident where liberal societies need to intervene to prevent groups from violating the individual rights of their members. Even when this intervention is legitimate, it is often justified on the basis of abstract principles which are generally misunderstood and tend to spur even further intercultural conflict. Needless to say, the habitat-nation is not immune to the challenges of diversity. The ecoliberal principles of justice nonetheless allow the political community to incorporate at the same time individual autonomy and the embeddedness of inhabitants, who are not mere abstract citizens but beings-in-the-world with legitimate and diverse vital aspirations in the spheres of life, well-being, sociability and culture. In a habitat-nation, inhabitants are not integrated into the same political community by virtue of a shared culture (nationalism), nor by virtue of a supposed neutrality of the state in relation to society (liberalism). If inhabitants form a single community, it is because they share the common good of sustainability of cohabitation, even when they do not share in the same degree a particular language, religion or other relevant cultural habits. Of course, a certain mutuality of cultural habits will help to sustain the social community, to the extent that it strengthens the ties of reciprocity and friendship between its members. This mutuality of cultural habits, however, is not postulated as an essential attribute of the political community. There is nothing to prevent a pluriethnic society from constituting itself as a habitat-nation, regardless of the specific difficulties that it may find in its actual political articulation. Whatever their culture, all human inhabitants already share by virtue of an almost identical genetic inheritance many fundamental habits, such as autonomy, reciprocity and friendship. It is on these habits, rather than on the abstract notion of moral personality, that the principles of justice which regulate the habitat-nation are founded. These principles establish clear limits to the demands of the different groups and individuals that make up the philial society, whether they are minorities or the majority, such as the respect for individual freedoms or the condition that public care should be to the greatest benefit of the community as a whole. Of course, the different philial groups will inevitably tend to promote their partial interests over the interests of other groups, sometimes even in a confrontational manner. Rather than being weakened, the habitat-nation is actually strengthened by this social dynamic, which reflects the systemic and complex nature of cohabitation. In this sense, we should perhaps conceive philial society as an ecosystem, formed by a mosaic of social groups organised at different levels of integration. These groups are irreducibly diverse and may hold antagonistic or conflictual relations, but they all depend on each other and share, when it is a real ecopolitical community, the aim of sustaining their common habitation. As long as the institutions of the habitat-nation ensure that no individual or group is able to bend the principles of justice on its own interest, the diversity of philial society is not a threat but an ecological richness that the political community would do well to preserve.

It is clear, in any case, that the model of the nation-state is unable to give a satisfactory response to the ethnic and cultural diversity of contemporary societies, even when it is articulated on the basis of liberal principles. There is just no way to reconcile the abstractness of these principles (moral personality) with the particularism of the political community (nation-state). This contradiction inevitably leads to double standards and to the good measure of bad faith that characterises many Western policies. We should not forget that liberal principles are not able to justify by themselves the existence of any political community organised within the boundaries of a state or a nation, much less when these boundaries are the product of such illiberal dynamics as wars of conquest, royal weddings or colonisation. Unfortunately, the alternative of a political community that would embrace the whole of humanity, or the whole world, is fatally naive. If this global community is supposed to be a regime of rights and duties, without an effective democratic articulation, the future citizens of the world, the *cosmopolites*, will have no more political potential than the visitors to a club of which they are not members. If the intention on the other hand is to develop a real political community at the global level, with an effective democratic articulation, then these *cosmopolites* will never see the light of day and will continue to deliberate amongst the Olympian gods, the Valkyrie, and the Hobbits.

This does not mean of course that the institutions and mechanisms of global coordination are not necessary, even indispensable. In an increasingly interdependent world, there are many social and ecological problems that cannot be tackled effectively at the state level, often not even at a regional or continental level. Global organisms are not, however, the panacea that cosmopolitans tend to describe. Bureaucracy, inefficiency and a disregard for local communities are serious shortcomings of the United Nations system, even in those areas where its action is essential. In the name of a universal conception of human rights or ecological sustainability, the teams of international experts often create more problems than they solve, particularly when they fail to take into account the conditions of habitation and the particular habits of the inhabitants. Policies that ended up being highly detrimental such as the "green revolution" have been nonetheless pursued on the basis of superior scientific principles, simply because their promoters had the prestige and the global resources to impose them in spite of the opposition of local inhabitants. Of course, we should not idealise the local communities either. They often have partial interests that do not recognise, for example, dynamics like the tragedy of the commons. But these communities stem in many cases from processes of adaptation to the habitat which have allowed them to develop habits and forms of habitation that only a patronising or neocolonialist attitude could ignore. Even in those cases where international coordination is justified by the systemic or global nature of the problem, the solutions should never be sought away from the inhabitants. On the contrary, meaningful political communities should always participate in the design and implementation of any policy that may affect them, in so far as they alone are legitimised and capable of effectively managing their own habitat.

The habitat-nation is not an isolated political unit, but one of the levels of integration that make up the global ecosystem that some have called Gaia. Other levels of integration with which the habitat-nation has to coordinate itself are the local or sectoral communities of philial society, as well as supranational, continental or global organisations. However, all these levels are not equivalent. The habitat-nation is the legitimate articulation of the community of free inhabitants, in so far as it alone is able to guarantee through democratic means the social and ecological sustainability of cohabitation. In this sense, the ecopolitical notion of inhabitant does not exclude any project of supranational, even universal citizenship, as long as it respects the legitimacy of the habitat-nation in the sphere of the effective political community. In classical terms, one may say that inhabitants are *polites* of their habitat-nation, notwithstanding the fact that they might exercise as well their rights and duties as *cives* of a larger political unit. The formation of habitat-nations may in fact strengthen the project of continental, even global integration. Not only does the size of ecopolitical communities facilitate cooperation between nations, but they already include this cooperation as one of their founding principles. Unlike the nation-state, founded on the substantial notion of sovereignty, the habitat-nation is founded on the sustainability of cohabitation, which is by nature relational and systemic. The social and biological communities that constitute the habitat-nation could never sustain themselves apart from other communities, given that all natural and social systems of the planet are tightly linked by multiple and complex interdependencies. Some of these interdependencies, politically articulated through the multilateral institutions and organisations, could actually strengthen the ties of cooperation between habitat-nations and significantly contribute to reduce international conflicts. A world where the model of the habitat-nation would be widespread, instead of the current world of nation-states, would not only be more peaceful, more democratic and more sustainable, but it would also gain in social and ecological resilience. Large nation-states, like large oak trees, may seem solid and stable; but a strong gust of wind can easily uproot them and leave them lying on the ground. The habitat-nation is more like the reed, capable of bending with the wind and surviving the most violent of storms. In a planet threatened by serious systemic risks, the articulation of global, continental, national and local governance requires democratic, flexible and lasting solutions. The sustainability of the habitat-world requires, perhaps necessarily, the constitution of a world of habitat-nations.

10 The Future of Habitat-nations

The theory of the habitat-nation that I have exposed in this book would make no sense if it did not aspire to have some influence on current debates. I hope to have shown the need and the possibility of advancing a political project that would have the model of the habitat-nation as its institutional framework, overcoming the dire straits between a dysfunctional nation-state and the cosmopolitan reverie. Let us accept then that a community of free inhabitants is a worthwhile political aim; but how do we go about to make it happen? The fact is that we are still living in a world of nation-states. Even universally-minded organisations such as the United Nations are grounded on a system of sovereign states, rather than nations. Similarly, the large continental units such as the European Union have been basically built up, in spite of some attempts to reinforce regionalism and supranational citizenship, on the basis of interstate coordination. Not to speak of the large and very large states, which of course not only reject the idea of an ecologically and socially meaningful political community, but they employ all the instruments of state power and the ideology of the nation-state to thwart its emergence. In such a context, and assuming that it is a desirable objective, how may we achieve in practice a world of habitat-nations?

Here, I will only consider the situation in Europe and North America. This is certainly a questionable choice, which contributes to perpetuate the all-too-common Eurocentric prejudice and tends to forget that there are many potential habitat-nations in other continents as well. From the point of view of efficacy, nevertheless, it is hard to imagine how the transformation of current geopolitical structures could be initiated from any other cultural area than the West. Not only because it is here where the ideology and the structure of the nation-state have their origin, but also because at present it is still the dominant economic, political and military region. Of course, this region is far from homogeneous, nor does it have very clearly defined boundaries. In order to simplify my analysis, I will concentrate exclusively on Europe (leaving aside northern Africa, western Asia, the Middle East, the Caucasus and other Russian-influenced areas), as well as on North America (leaving aside all Central America and the Caribbean, except Mexico). What is important, in any case, is not so much the incorporation of a particular country or region, but the general direction of the movement that I am trying to project here, even if very schematically.

To begin, we should realise that there are already in the world a considerable number of states that are on an appropriate scale for a habitat-nation (a socially and ecologically meaningful community). Some of these states, basically in northern Europe (Sweden, Norway, Finland, Iceland, the Netherlands and Denmark), also have institutions which approach the ecopolitical ideal quite closely, even if they could certainly benefit from reforms aimed at strengthening their philial societies and improving their sustainability. Beyond these quasi habitat-nations, the European states that have an adequate size but not the institutions of a habitat-nation are perhaps the ones who could advance faster towards the ecopolitical model. Some of these small nations (Czech Republic, Ireland, Hungary, Slovakia, Croatia, Slovenia, Lithuania, Latvia, Estonia) are already moving more or less effectively in this direction and they could join with relative ease the group of the quasi habitat-nations. Other small nations (Serbia, Greece, Portugal, Bulgaria, Moldova, Albania, Kosovo, Cyprus, Macedonia, Montenegro), in spite of having the right size, will not be able to make this transition without transforming in depth their political, economic and social institutions. There also a handful of European states (Austria, Belgium, Switzerland, Bosnia-Herzegovina) that have the right size, but are ecologically or socially too fragmented to evolve as habitat-nations, even where their institutional models, particularly in the case of Switzerland, are already ecopolitically sound. Finally, we should mention the independent microstates (Monaco, Andorra, San Marino, Vatican, Liechtenstein, Luxembourg, Malta), which are too small to become effective ecopolitical communities but could persist with little or no change in a future world of habitat-nations.

Concentrating on Europe, therefore, we find a group of 6 states that are almost habitat-nations (group A: average population of 7 million inhabitants), another group of 9 states that could develop relatively quickly the institutions of the habitat-nation (group B: average population of 5 million inhabitants), and a third group of 10 states with an adequate dimension but in need of profound institutional reforms in order to become habitat-nations (group C: average population of 5 million inhabitants). These three groups of small nations with their own state (A, B and C) make up together 47% of the surface area and 25% of the total population of Europe. Additionally, the 4 small states with a complex internal structure and the 7 independent microstates cover 4% of the surface area and include 6% of the European population. The remaining surface area (49%) and population (69%) corresponds to the large European states: Germany, France, United Kingdom, Italy, Spain, Poland and Romania (average population of 53 million inhabitants).

In summary, it could be argued that Europe is currently divided in two blocks: the large states (49% of the territory, 69% of the population, 16% of the states) and the small nations (51% of the territory, 31% of the population, 84% of the states). There is no doubt that this situation is seriously hampering the normal development of the European Union, in so far as the interstate institutions of governance (Council, Commission) need to be articulated from clearly asymmetrical political units. While the project of a unified Europe has continued to advance, following in particular the consolidation of the single market and the single currency, it seems increasingly evident that effective power in the European institutions lies in the large states, especially in Germany and France. The resistance of the smaller states to the development of this Franco-German axis is one of the main focuses of tension within the European Union, which is thus forced to stagger ahead under a permanent dynamic of negotiation, compromise and barter. As a result, the more ambitious aims of a virtual confederation of states are indefinitely postponed.

The only realistic solution to this problem is the geopolitical rebalancing of the different units that make up the European Union (or Europe as a whole). This could be done either by unifying the small states into large states following the Westphalian logic (an option that is clearly not feasible in practice), or by breaking up the large states into small states. This last option has been on the table for some time and has inspired, albeit not in such stark terms, the institutional project of the Europe of the Regions. While the idea of a Europe divided into regional units is sensible enough, its conception as a gradual process of decentralisation in the hands of the nation-states, hoping there will come a time in which the European Union could be structured on the basis of regional units of comparable size, is just too naive. The absence of a theoretical framework capable of replacing the ideology of the nation-state has meant in practice that large states have continued to apply a top-down regionalisation based on administrative criteria, while some already quite homogeneous nations such as Ireland or Greece were almost forced to regionalise themselves in order to comply with the Cartesian conceptions of the bureaucrats in Brussels or Strasbourg. To the extent that the political institutions of the European Union continued to be controlled by the states, despite the usual rhetoric of europhiles, small nations have tried as best they could to preserve their decreasing sphere of sovereignty, at the same time that large states tried as best they could to increase their influence, in a game of pure political and demographic force that goes right against the essence of the European project. The Europe of the Regions, conceived from foggy ideas, is thus little more than a vast technocratic chimera where the most diverse interests meet, but which ends up always ruled by the usual three or four.

Hence, it is essential that the progress towards a Europe of the habitat-nations does not fall into the traps of regionalism. The aim is not to regionalise Europe, but to renationalise it. Such renationalisation should not be based on the model of the nation-state but on the habitat-nation, an ecologically and socially meaningful community founded on the sustainability of cohabitation and on philiocratic political institutions. It is necessary, therefore, to initiate a transition towards a new Europe of the habitat-nations, overcoming once and for all the ideology of the nation-state and the concentration of power in the large Westphalian states. This process will never stem from the European institutions, much less of course from the large states themselves. Neither will it originate in the small nations with state, which lack clear incentives to promote such a sweeping change, even if they would certainly benefit from giving their full support to a rebalancing of the geopolitical map of Europe. Only the small nations that are still integrated in large European states due to various historical and political circumstances may actually be able to initiate the process that ends up transforming the Europe of the nation-states into the Europe of the habitat-nations.

The group of small nations without state (group N) includes all those political communities that have an adequate size and enough internal cohesion to become habitat-nations, even if they lack state structures or well-developed ecopolitical institutions. Once they become independent states, some of these nations could be classified under group A (together with the nations that have the best institutional quality), although most would probably fit better in group B (with the nations that need to improve their institutions) or even in group C (with the nations that need to implement much deeper changes in their institutional framework). Given that none of the nations in this group has yet a state of its own, even if most have their own political and administrative structures within the regional or federal organisation of the large state to which they belong, it is somewhat difficult to identify them with too much precision. It should be remarked that not all regions of the large states have the potential or the will to constitute themselves as habitat-nations. Some are mere administrative divisions, which have been defined without taking into account the ecological or social cohesion of their inhabitants. Many others, even if they constitute potentially meaningful communities, are still very much tied to the ideology that justifies the existence of the large state. In the present context, therefore, only some of these communities could effectively constitute themselves as habitat-nations, adopting state structures comparable to the ones in groups A, B or C. Amongst these, there are several small nations that will hardly engage in a process of secession that would imply breaking up the large state, no matter how attractive the alternative may seem. Others could possibly engage in such a process, but they will never assume the initiative and would rather wait for others to take the first step.

Only a handful of small nations without state would therefore be in a condition to achieve right away their independence, becoming in effect the forefront of this movement towards a Europe of habitat-nations.

In view of the diversity of options and strategies facing these potential habitat-nations, the process of breaking up the large states is likely to unfold, if at all, by successive steps. An early group of pioneers (Catalonia, Scotland, the Basque Country, Flanders) may constitute themselves as states in the very short term. If these processes of secession are successful, others would probably follow (Wales, Northern Ireland, Corsica, Brittany, Lombard, Venice, Piedmont, Sardinia, Sicily, the Balearic Islands, Valencia, the Canary Islands, Galicia, Bavaria). After this second wave, the geopolitical structure of Europe would have become much more balanced, with 7 large states (40% of the territory, 55% of the population) and 54 small nations (60% of the territory, 45% of the population). From this point forward, the scenario of a general reorganisation of the European Union, with the breaking up of the large states into smaller bioregional units, would no longer seem so implausible. The German Länder, for instance, could evolve quite rapidly to take advantage of the new territorial structure, easily adopting ecopolitical structures and institutions. This process would definitely contribute to settling down the fears of a great Germany, particularly amongst the remaining large states. Even then, the reorganisation of states like Italy, Spain,

England, and particularly France, marked by their strong centralist traditions, would still pose some difficulties and generate a fair amount of resistance. In the long run, however, the pressure of the small nations and the obvious benefits of a Europe of habitat-nations would most likely tip the scales and force even the most Jacobin of states to break up into more efficient and democratic units. At the end of this process, Europe could be formed by approximately 90 states, with an average population of 6 million inhabitants and an average surface area of 55,000 square kilometres. The economic, social and political differences between these states would still be significant, but the institutions of continental governance could become more fluid and fair, contributing to reinforce the ties of solidarity between the different habitat-nations. There is no doubt, in any case, that this Europe of the habitat-nations would be more democratic, more prosperous and more balanced than today's Europe of the nation-states.

Needless to say, all these projections are only hypothetical. If the Europeans themselves, and in particular the citizens of the large states, which are the ones most harmed by their inefficient, undemocratic and unfair institutions, do not mobilise to demand a transformation of the political framework, we will continue more or less like today. If they did mobilise, however, Europeans have in their hands the construction of a new Europe of habitat-nations. They only need to leave behind the old republican myths and their loyalty to large modern states, which are no longer able to guarantee justice, but have become in fact the infrastructure of injustice itself. The independence of some Western nations with the capacity to rapidly evolve into ecopolitical communities, such as Scotland, Catalonia, Flanders or the Basque Country, should thus have the support of all Europeans, not only in the small nations with state or in other nations that aspire to independence, but even in the large states from which they would like to separate. It is not a question of dividing, but of creating new, more inclusive and democratic political communities. Large states, beyond the role they might have played in the process of modernisation, are no longer able to offer a framework of cohabitation and prosperity, much less of solidarity. While the small nations of Europe advance in the path of well-being and social justice, the large states founder like old Diplodocus in the swamps of globalisation, hardly able to sustain themselves on the ideology of power and the vaporous mirages of history. It is difficult to understand why any European would want to live today in a large state, when it is so obvious that a community of free inhabitants can only evolve in the context of a small nation. Even those who hold fast to the dreams of a universal democratic community or to the idea of a great European state should realise that a politically unified Europe will never be a democratic Europe. At best, it will be an extended regime of rights and duties, built on the basis of citizens as fictitious as the bridges depicted in the Euro notes. The only framework that may allow a sufficient level of political participation is the ecologically and socially meaningful community, the habitat-nation. And only a Europe of habitat-nations may be able to fulfil the aspirations of those Europeans who dream of a more united and democratic continent.

The ecopolitical project is certainly not restricted to the boundaries of the European continent. Also the United States, Canada, even Mexico, amongst other countries in the world, could clearly benefit from a geopolitical reorganisation founded on socially and ecologically meaningful communities while strengthening the ties of continental cooperation. The American case is, nonetheless, quite different from the European one. In some ways, the transition towards an America of habitat-nations is easier, in so far as there are no large states with deep historical roots, but three very large and highly decentralised territorial units with a tradition of active grassroots democracy (at least in the United States and Canada). At the same time, however, this transition is more difficult due to the absence of social communities linked with the different habitats, as these traditional communities, the so-called Indians, have been displaced, marginalised, assimilated or directly exterminated in the not so distant past. Consequently, the strategies that could lead to the formation of habitat-nations in the American context tend to be more social than strictly political, leaving aside the exceptional case of Quebec, whose independence may indeed spark deeper changes in the whole continent. The vigour of the bioregionalist movement in the United States is perhaps another factor that may promote the development of an America of habitat-nations. But first, bioregionalists should probably renounce the deep ecological mysticism that often inspires them and embrace a more politically sensible conception of the community, one in which all inhabitants may be able to find their place. In any case, the outcome of an ecopolitical movement in the United States, which is no doubt the key country, is quite uncertain given that the economic, political and social structure of the liberal federation of states is still firmly grounded and draws widespread support amongst a heterogeneous population characterised by fairly weak philial bonds. If such a transition would successfully begin in Europe, perhaps there could be a contagion effect that would give an impulse to a similar movement in North America. But even then, the reorganisation of a post-colonial geopolitical structure to create habitat-nations with a minimum degree of ecological and social coherence poses very serious challenges.

European habitat-nations must of course face, at least in part, similar challenges. Earlier, I took for granted that the borders of these new habitat-nations would correspond to the current states and regions. Needless to say, this is a simplification, even if not a particularly grievous one in the case of Europe.

We should not forget that the habitat-nation is theoretically defined by the coincidence of a biological and a social community. This means that we cannot, for example, organise the geopolitical structure of Europe by simply taking the 70 ecoregions from the Digital Map of European Ecological Regions (DMEER), compiled by a team of experts for the European Environment Agency. These regions may provide us with a starting point to determine the ecological coherence of the different habitat-nations, but they cannot determine their boundaries, in so far as we still need to take into account the question of social coherence. In Europe, the geographical limits of small states and regions already correspond, albeit approximately, to the limits of culturally and historically meaningful communities. Certainly, there are quite a few cases of disputed borders, minority enclaves and divided communities, which derive in general from the political and military competition between large states in the course of history. In the context of a democratic reorganisation of European geopolitics, many of these conflicts could be peacefully solved by allowing the social communities themselves to choose the habitat-nation that they would rather be part of. Besides these adjustments, however, the underlying territorial structure of Europe (small nations and regions), to the extent that it responds to dynamics of coadaptation that are relatively ancient, implies already in one way or another a significant degree of social and even ecological cohesion.

The situation in America is indeed very different. As any map will show, the majority of states and provinces that make up the United States, Canada and Mexico have been traced with a ruler, without taking into account the boundaries of the underlying social or biological communities. In so far as these communities have been deeply disrupted by the substitution of the original inhabitants with a population of European immigrants and the accelerated exploitation of their natural resources, it is rather far-fetched to speak of social or ecological coherence in the case of North American states. In this context, it is quite understandable that bioregionalists should propose a profound reorganisation of internal borders, according for instance to the 182 ecoregions in level III of the Map of Ecological Regions of North America (Commission for Environmental Cooperation). Even here, however, habitat-nations cannot be founded exclusively on their degree of ecological coherence, but need to take into account social coherence as well, no matter how fragile or recent it happens to be. Lacking any meaningful criteria to establish beforehand where these boundaries may lie in practice, we could try projecting the ecopolitical organisation of the North American continent based on the current states and federated provinces of the United States, Canada and Mexico. From this point of view, an America of habitat-nations might be formed by a total of 96 states, with an average population of 4.7 million inhabitants and an average surface area of

215,000 square kilometres. It is important not to forget, however, that the American territorial structure is likely to undergo many more rearrangements than the European one before attaining a stable and meaningful ecopolitical organisation.

While obviously hypothetical, these projections reflect the formation of two large continental units, Europe and North America, with a similar total population (EU: 541 million; NA: 450 million) and a territorial composition that is also comparable (EU: 90 states with an average of 6 million inhabitants; NA: 96 states with an average of 4.7 million inhabitants). Considering the differences in extension between the two continents (EU: 5 million square kilometres; NA: 20 million square kilometres), the habitat-nations in one case and the other will significantly differ in their average size (EU: 55.000 square kilometres; NA: 215.000 square kilometres), as well as average density (EU: 108 inhabitants per square kilometre; NA: 22 inhabitants per square kilometre). This divergence should not affect, in any case, the sustainability of the corresponding habitat-nations, even if it implies that the forms of habitation developed on both sides of the Atlantic may be somewhat different.

The advantages of such geopolitical arrangement, both for each individual habitat-nation and for the continent as a whole, should already be clear enough. As I have tried to establish throughout this book, small-scale political units like the habitat-nations tend to have more social cohesion and more democratic institutions, as well as lower transaction costs, than larger states. At the same time, the coordination between these small units at the level of their own continental confederations ensures that the most onerous public goods, such as defence, internal market or foreign policy, could attain a sufficient and economic scale. Moreover, this coordination should be more effective than in current supranational structures, given that all the units would have equivalent dimensions and the same constitutional foundations. It would thus be easier to devise and implement programmes of regional solidarity that could benefit the least advantaged nations or those with structural problems without submitting them to the stronger or richer nations of the continent. If one of these habitat-nations would suffer an antidemocratic involution or threatened in some way the stability of the continental confederation, the other nations could intervene to restablish the ecopolitical institutions of the rogue state. Once again, this would not be perceived as the imposition of a large state over its smaller neighbours, but as the result of democratic processes conducted by a plurality of states with equal powers. In such a system of egalitarian habitat-nations, trade would naturally tend to increase, especially at the continental level. At the same time, the negative effects of this trade on the sustainability of each individual habitat-nation should be largely diminished, as the ecopolitical institutions of the nations themselves would forestall the overexploitation of natural resources. With stable economies, solid philial ties and dynamic societies, these continental confederations would also be strengthened against potential threats from large political units that have not yet developed ecopolitical institutions. Furthermore, their resilience against systemic risks such as climate change or food supply crises would also be significantly improved. In so far as these continental confederations would be regulated by philiocratic institutions, their foreign policy would respond to criteria of justice and sustainability, rather than to imperial ambitions. A Europe and an America of habitat-nations should therefore promote changes at the scale of the whole planet that would tend towards the formation of a true world of habitat-nations.

It is very easy to dismiss these kind of visions as mere fancy or utopian reverie. There is no denying that the path leading to a world such as the one I am projecting here (after all, projecting is free) is filled with obstacles, traps, precipices and all sorts of hazards that would test the faith of any prophet. And yet the vision of a world of habitat-nations, which is not a new proposal but the articulation of ideas that have been around at least since Plato, is not more utopian than the League of Nations or the United Nations. Unlike these projects, however, the ecopolitical proposal is not grounded on the abstract notion of moral personality, but on the realities of habitation and the ties that bind the inhabitants to the rest of inhabitants and to the habitat they all share.

The Future of Habitat-nations

No matter how far away it may seem, a world of habitat-nations is more easily attainable for humans than any form of universal democracy. The world's citizens, the *cosmopolites*, are bodiless, lifeless creatures, pure creations of the mind that are unlikely to see the light of day or breath the planet's air. Inhabitants, on the contrary, are individuals who already exist in the world; they are you, they are me, they are he or she, they are the aspen and the starling, they are all of us, living beings who inhabit some place in this earth, within a biological community and often also within a social community. The humanist idea of the moral person, conceived as a kind of soul that floats over the world, too often prevents us from recognising all the interdependencies that bind us to our habitat and to the rest of inhabitants. Historically, it has also prevented us from developing inclusive political communities, founded on the sustainability of cohabitation. These communities are not unreachable utopian islands, but forms of institutional organisation that are perfectly realisable under our natural conditions. In order to advance towards this world, we just need to begin by organising our own home, our own habitat-nation. Only in so far as we, the inhabitants, assume the responsibility for our own habitat, can we expect that some day, if the odds are in our favour, this larger home that is the earth will also be, and for all, inhabitable.

*

Sources and References

I have made my best efforts to reduce to the bare minimum the references and quotes in the main body of the text, in order not to distract the reader with names, page numbers and editions. To compensate, I will briefly comment here on the main references that support my arguments, as well as giving the source of the quotes that appear throughout the book.

THE BEAR AND THE STORK: A FABLE

For a good account of Lithuania's role in the dissolution of the Soviet Union, I would recommend reading Richard Krickus' *Showdown: The Lithuanian Rebellion and the Breakup of the Soviet Empire* (Brassey's, 1997).

221

HABIT OR THE ANIMAL

On the animality of humans, Mary Midgley's *Beast and Man: The Roots of Human Nature* (Routledge, 1978) is a classic worth reviewing. In *The Blank Slate: The Modern Denial of Human Nature* (Penguin, 2002), Steven Pinker discusses in detail some of the questions raised in this chapter such as the motivations of human behaviour. Another book that surveys the same ground from a slightly different perspective, while offering a fascinating description of the cultural and biological coevolution of humans, is *Not By Genes Alone: How Culture Transformed Human Evolution* (University of Chicago Press, 2005), by Peter Richerson and Robert Boyd. An in-depth account of the experiments and theoretical models that underpin my discussion of the prosocial inclinations of humans will be found in *A Cooperative Species: Human Reciprocity and Its Evolution* (Princeton University Press, 2011), by economists Samuel Bowles and Herbert Gintis. I have partly derived the notion of habit from the insights of two French anthropologists, Marcel Mauss (see his essay on *"Les techniques du corps"*, 1934) and especially Pierre Bourdieu, who elaborated the key sociological concept of *habitus* (see for example, *Outline of a Theory of Practice*, Cambridge University Press, 1972). These notions are developed by Tim Ingold in *The Perception of the Environment: Essays on Livelihood, Dwelling and Skill* (Routledge, 2000).

HABITATION OR DWELLING

On the issues of human ecology raised in this chapter, I have mostly relied on *Human Ecology: Biocultural Adaptations in Human Communities* by Holger Schutkowski (Springer, 2006), but there are many good introductions to the subject such as Emilio Moran's *Human Adaptability: An Introduction to Ecological Anthropology* (Westview, 2000). The influence of geographic and historical factors on the processes of human habitation is the main storyline of Jared Diamond's *Guns, Germs and Steel: A Short History of Everybody for the Last 13,000 Years* (W. W. Norton, 1997). An excellent textbook which develops in depth the ecological concepts too briefly discussed in the chapter is *Ecology: From Individuals to Ecosystems* (Wiley-Blackwell, 2006, 4th edition), by Michael Begon, Colin Townsend and John Harper. A more accessible discussion of these same concepts, together with a very clear exposition of the general problems of sustainability, may be found in Gerald Marten's *Human Ecology: Basic Concepts for Sustainable Development* (Earthscan, 2001). There are many other texts such as Clive Ponting's *A New Green History of the World: The Environment and the Collapse of Great Civilizations* (Penguin, 2007), which cover the not so exemplary ecological record of humans throughout history. The term "tragedy of the commons" is now quite widespread, but was originally coined by Garret Hardin and has been analysed from the perspective of economics by Elinor Ostrom in *Governing the Commons: The Evolution of Institutions for Collective Action* (Cambridge University Press, 1990). My comments on the possible collapse of our civilisation owe a special debt to Joseph Tainter's *The Collapse of Complex Societies* (Cambridge University Press, 1988). I should perhaps clarify the indirect reference to Thomas Malthus' theory of population (*An Essay on the Principle of Population*, 1798). Finally, the Pascalian wager refers of course to Blaise Pascal's *Thoughts* (1669; English edition: Greenwood Press, 1978).

INHABITANTS OR DWELLERS

The Western idea of the subject has been criticised with notable depth, but not so much clarity, by Martin Heidegger. As shown by the concept of "being-in-the-world" discussed in the chapter, I have been enlightened in many ways by his thought, particularly by *Being and Time* (1927; English edition: Harper, 1962). Aristotle's quotes are mainly from his *Politics,* in particular from books I and III. For the English text I have mostly relied on C. D. C. Reeve's edition (Hackett Publishing, 1998), although I have slightly modified some of his translations. There is a vast literature on the ancient notion of citizenship, both in Greece and Rome, but a mandatory stop is J. G. A. Pocock's brilliant essay "The Ideal of Citizenship Since Classical

Times" (*Queen's Quarterly*, 1992). A more factual approach to the history of citizenship may be found in Peter Riesenberg's *Citizenship in the Western Tradition: Plato to Rousseau* (University of North Carolina Press, 1992). It is from this book that I have also drawn Epictetus' quote (*Discourses*). Jean Bodin's theory of sovereignty is mainly developed in *The Six Books of the Republic* (1576). The classic political works of John Locke (*Two Treatises of Government*, 1690) and Jean-Jacques Rousseau (*Le Contrat social*, 1762) are quite well-known and do not need much introduction. For the English translation of the latter, I have used Susan Dunn's edition of *The Social Contract and The First and Second Discourses* (Yale University Press, 2002). The U.S. Supreme Court's quote is taken from the case *Trop vs. Dulles* (1958). There are many books that analyse, more or less critically, the political foundations and limits of current systems of representative democracy. A good anthology on the subject is *The Democracy Sourcebook*, edited by Robert Dahl, Ian Shapiro and José Antonio Cheibub (MIT Press, 2003). On the empirical evidence behind some of my claims about the political distrust of citizens in contemporary democracies, see Russell Dalton's *Democratic Challenges, Democratic Choices: The Erosion of Political Support in Advanced Industrial Democracies* (Oxford University Press, 2004). The idea of a universal grammar was originally advanced by Noam Chomsky in his influential *Aspects of the Theory of Syntax* (MIT Press, 1965).

The debate between liberals and communitarians is well covered by Stephen Mulhall and Adam Swift in *Liberals and Communitarians* (Blackwell, 1992). In this same context, the most consistent critique of the liberal subject was perhaps elaborated by Michael Sandel in *Liberalism and the Limits of Justice* (Cambridge University Press, 1982). The description of Olympus is taken from Homer's *Odyssey*, book VI. The question of animal rights and the extension of moral consideration beyond human beings is discussed in Peter Singer's *The Expanding Circle: Ethics, Evolution, and Moral Progress* (Princeton University Press, 1981). A noteworthy, albeit not fully convincing approach to the theoretical problems of extending the notion of justice to non-humans may be found in Brian Baxter's *A Theory of Ecological Justice* (Routledge, 2005). Last, but certainly not least, John Rawls' theory is mainly developed in his *A Theory of Justice* (Harvard University Press, 1999 [1971], revised edition), which is arguably the most significant contribution to liberal political theory in the last century and is the object of further discussion in the following chapters.

HABITAT OR THE NATION

The concept of "minimal state" is developed in Robert Nozick's *Anarchy, State, and Utopia* (Basic Books, 1974). Needless to say, there is a huge and ever growing literature on the nation and nationalism. Good introductions to contemporary theoretical debates are Umut Ozkirimli's *Theories of Nationalism: A Critical Introduction* (Palgrave Macmillan, 2010, 2nd edition) and Jonathan Hearn's *Rethinking Nationalism: A Critical Introduction* (Palgrave, 2006). *When is the Nation? Towards an Understanding of Theories of Nationalism*, edited by Atsuko Ichijo and Gordana Uzelac (Routledge, 2005), is another interesting volume with concise and contrasted contributions by the main theoreticians in the field. For an exposition of the principles and applications of ecoregional mapping, one should look no further than Robert G. Bailey's *Ecosystem Geography: From Ecoregions to Sites* (Springer, 2009, 2nd edition). The WWF map of the world's ecoregions may be found in the Internet: worldwildlife.org/biomes. The quote is taken from the article "Terrestrial Ecoregions of the World: A New Map of Life on Earth" (*Bioscience*, 2001), written by the team of scientists behind the project. An overview of bioregional management, quite free from bioregionalist lore, may be found in David Brunckhorst's *Bioregional Planning: Resource Management Beyond the New Millennium* (Routledge, 2000). My comments on economic efficiency as a criterion to determine the optimal size of habitat-nations are based on Alberto Alesina and Enrico Spolaore's *The Size of Nations* (MIT Press, 2003). The United Nations definition of sustainable development was initially put forward in the "Report of the World

Commission on Environment and Development", General Assembly Resolution 42/187, 11 December 1987. Aldo Leopold's quote is from *A Sand County Almanac* (Oxford University Press, 1949) and Carol Gilligan's from *In a Different Voice: Psychological Theory and Women's Development* (Harvard University Press, 1982). The distinction between "civic nations" and "ethnic nations" was first proposed by Hans Kohn and subscribed amongst others by Ernest Gellner. Since then, it has been systematically undermined by critics, but continues to exercise a significant influence in political discourse. My analysis takes some cues from Walker Connor's path-breaking essay "Nation-building or nation-destroying?" (*World Politics*, 1972). I am also particularly indebted to Will Kymlicka's compelling reflections on the dynamics of majority and minority nations in the context of modern nation-states, for example in his *Multicultural Citizenship: A Liberal Theory of Minority Rights* (Clarendon, 1995). The concept of "banal nationalism" was coined by Michael Billig in his essay *Banal Nationalism* (Sage, 1995). A good survey on the issue of ethnicity, particularly in relation to the nation, may be found in Thomas Eriksen's *Ethnicity and Nationalism: Anthropological Perspectives* (Pluto Press, 2010, 3rd edition). The genetic or socio-biological explanation of the nation to which I allude in the chapter was first proposed by Pierre van den Berghe in *The Ethnic Phenomenon* (Praeger, 1981). The reference to George Orwell's *Animal Farm* (Secker and Warburg, 1945) paraphrases one of the pigs' commandments: "All animals are equal, but some animals are more equal than others". A good monograph on the subject of friendship is Daniel Hruschka's *Friendship: Development, Ecology, and Evolution of a Relationship* (University of California Press, 2010). The last quotes from Aristotle will be found in book VIII of *Nicomachean Ethics*. For the English translation, I have relied on Roger Crisp's edition (Cambridge University Press, 2004). An eminent critic of the political and moral implications of friendship's particularism is Lawrence Kohlberg (see for example his *Essays on Moral Development*, Harper & Row, 1984). Edward O. Wilson's hypothesis was initially exposed in *Biophilia* (Harvard University Press, 1984).

ECOLIBERAL PRINCIPLES OF JUSTICE

The overarching reference for this chapter is the already mentioned *A Theory of Justice* by John Rawls. For the communitarian critique, beyond the previously quoted references, one should probably read Charles Taylor's essays, for example his *Philosophy and the Human Sciences: Philosophical Papers, vol. II* (Cambridge University Press, 1985). For the idea of moral personality and its ethical justification, see Immanuel Kant's *Groundwork of the Metaphysic of Morals* (1785; English edition: Yale University Press, 2002). The old concept of the "great chain of being" is covered in depth by Arthur O. Lovejoy in *The Great*

Chain of Being: A Study of the History of an Idea (Harvard University Press, 1936). The key empirical study on the relationship between interpersonal trust and political legitimacy is Robert Putnam's *Making Democracy Work: Civic Traditions in Modern Italy* (Princeton University Press, 1993).

A COMMUNITY OF FREE INHABITANTS

The so-called elitist (or technocratic) theory of democracy was outlined by Joseph Schumpeter in his *Capitalism, Society and Democracy* (Harper & Bros, 1942). The question of democracy is of course a vast and widely open subject. For an excellent introduction, see David Held's *Models of Democracy* (Polity Press, 2006). In opposition to the theories of "competitive elitism", the need for more participatory forms of democracy was argued in a very convincing manner by Carole Pateman in her *Participation and Democratic Theory* (Cambridge University Press, 1970). For a more empirical and recent discussion, I would recommend *Democracy Transformed? Expanding Political Opportunities in Advanced Industrial Democracies*, by Bruce Cain, Russell Dalton and Susan Scarrow (Oxford University Press, 2003). James Madison's famous article, originally published in 1787, will be found in *The Federalist Papers*, together with other contributions by Alexander Hamilton and John Jay (Palgrave Macmillan, 2006).

John Stuart Mill's quote is taken from his *Considerations on Representative Government* (Parker, Son & Bourn, 1861). The distinction between consensual and majority systems of democracy was elaborated by Arend Lijphart in *Patterns of Democracy* (Yale University Press, 1999). Plato's classical critique of democracy, including his ship metaphor, will be found in the *Republic*, particularly in books VI and VIII. On the bureaucratic nature of modern political systems (and organisations in general), see Max Weber's classic analysis in *Economy and Society: An Outline of Interpretive Sociology* (1922; English edition: University of California Press, 1968). Robert Michels' 1911 scathing study of modern political parties has been translated to English in *Political Parties: A Sociological Study of the Oligarchical Tendencies of Modern Democracy* (Transaction Publishers, 1999). For the notion of the "fetish" of democracy and its criticism, see Friedrich Hayek's *The Road to Serfdom* (Routledge, 1976). A good place to review the proposals for a deliberative democracy is the collection of essays edited by Jon Elster in *Deliberative Democracy* (Cambridge University Press, 1998). For the critique of instrumental rationality and the concept of the "public sphere", see Jürgen Habermas' *The Theory of Communicative Action* (1981; English edition: Beacon Press, 1984, 1987, 2 volumes).

INHABITING THE WORLD

The typology of geopolitical units developed at the beginning of the chapter is inspired by Josep Maria Colomer's *Great Empires, Small Nations* (Routledge, 2007). Montesquieu's quote is taken from Book VIII, chapter 16, of *The Spirit of the Laws* (1748; English edition: T. Evans, 1777). A notorious case of global institutions undermining local communities and ecosystems is India's "green revolution", denounced by Vandana Shiva in *The Violence of the Green Revolution: Third World Agriculture, Ecology, and Politics* (Zed Books, 1991). The so-called "Gaia hypothesis" was mainly developed by James Lovelock in his *Gaia: A New Look at Life on Earth* (Oxford University Press, 1979).

THE FUTURE OF HABITAT-NATIONS

The solution of breaking up the large modern states into smaller units was advanced a long time ago in an unjustly ignored essay by Leopold Kohr, *The Breakdown of Nations* (Rinehart, 1957). Of course, the idea that states should be small is much older and could be traced all the way back to Plato's comments in book V of *The Laws*. The Digital Map of European Ecological Regions (DMEER) will be found in the European Environment Agency's webpage: eea.europa.eu. For the mapping of North American ecoregions, see the websites of the U. S. Environmental Protection Agency: epa.gov, or the Commission for Environmental Cooperation: cec.org. Additional maps to support the arguments of this chapter are included in the companion webpage to this book: habitat-nation.org, which of course you are invited to visit.

About the Author

Ignasi Ribó (Barcelona, 1971) is a Catalan writer. He is Doctor of Philosophy from the University of Sussex and holds graduate degrees in Business, Political Science and Literary Theory. He has published several novels in Catalan and Spanish, as well as academic essays on literary theory, politics and philosophy. Besides writing, he has worked in investment banking, international aid, consulting and teaching.

*

Also by Ignasi Ribó

Fiction
També somien els búfals
La ley de la gravedad
Polifemo
Mitrídates ha muerto
La palma y el laurel

Nonfiction
La teoria literària
De la indignació a la nació

*

You can visit his webpage at
www.ignasiribo.com

***

This is the first edition of
Habitat: The Ecopolitical Nation
by Ignasi Ribó.

It was published in print and electronic formats on
October 1, 2012.

Thank you for reading it.

***

www.ingramcontent.com/pod-product-compliance
Lightning Source LLC
Chambersburg PA
CBHW031428270326
41930CB00007B/612